THE POWER
OF TWO

THE POWER OF TWO

A NOVEL

By Robert (Bob) M. Parham, Jr.
and Jo Ann Walton Parham

This is dedicated
to our children
Sam, Terry and Danny,
and in memory of
Robert and Cindy,
who spent much of their
childhoods in Nigeria,
and to all who
loved Nigeria

ACKNOWLEDGEMENTS

This story has been in the making for many years and was
primarily done by Bob. Many people read, suggested, encouraged
and supported the writing. We are most thankful for their
participation in the effort to help people understand a few things
about Nigeria during the early to mid 1960s.

Among those who helped in various ways are Paul, Comfort
& Ruby Ebhomielen, Dr. Cornell Goerner, Norma Hoffman,
Dr. James & Jane Kimbrough, Louise Davis, Dr. Jann Aldredge
Clanton, Dr. Alan Powell, Jay & Joan Carter, Frances Ogle,
Mary Glazer, Jerri Simmons, Winnie Wyatt and Christine Wood.
A special help came from Dawn Allman, who prepared
the manuscript for publication.

TABLE OF CONTENTS

1 Great Anticipation 1

2 Horror Replaces Joy 10

3 Grandma's Grief 15

4 A Flight Begins 20

5 A Sad Morning 30

6 Found at Last 34

7 Broadening His Search 39

8 Unplanned Journey 45

9 The Lonely Hunt Continues 54

10 Safe at Last 61

11 Trip to Danbar 69

12 A Strange Place 78

13 Danger 88

14 A Place to Stay 90

15 Audu and Yahaya Meet 94

16 Unfortunate Contact 108

17 A Wise Woman 114

18 Yahaya Escapes Jail 118

19 Babies In Critical Condition 124

20 Two Coffins and a Letter 130

21 Despair or Peace 138

22 Venturing Further 144

23 An Important Purchase 153

24 A Fellow Villager Offers Help 159

25 Finally, Peace 168

   Epilogue 178

   About the Authors 181

Preface

With a four-month-old baby, Bob and Jo Ann Parham sailed to Nigeria to serve as missionaries. Four additional children joined their family during the more than 20 years they were involved with mission work in Nigeria.

They enjoyed many responsibilities, manifold blessings and great happiness. Their homes were in five diversified stations, among many different tribes, each with its own language and customs. Tasks varied. Bob's responsibilities included serving as an evangelist, agriculturalist, hospital business manager, school teacher and administrator. Jo Ann was a homemaker, school teacher, leader for the women's work, as well as a mother and supporting wife.

The characters, places, events, and even the cost of things in this story are imaginary, yet the story is the plain and simple truth. In Nigeria, meaningfulness and fulfillment in life are often best achieved by having children. What happens when a long-held tradition requires your dearest treasure? Will the heartfelt desire for a long-awaited child be strong enough to withstand the tribal pressure of a superstitious birth?

CHAPTER ONE

Great Anticipation

Laraba feels she has waited an eternity to have this baby. Will it be the son Audu longs for? Or will he finally give up on her? Will he send her away or take another wife? These thoughts consume her mind as she finishes the day's work on her farm. She begins her trek returning to the village. Looking back over her shoulders, she smiles as she glances over the tilled and planted soil. Going down the path, she considers the maize her farm will yield in a few weeks. She is happy and proud that her crop is full and rich, one of the best she has produced. Perhaps this is a good sign.

Halfway home, Laraba stops to enjoy the refreshment of the stream. Although the rainy season is ending, the water remains almost halfway up on each side of the banks. Now it slowly flows over the stones in the bottom.

Leaving her wrap on the ground, she walks out into the water. Leaning over, she cups her hands to bring water to her thirsty mouth. Since she doesn't have soap or a sponge, she can't take a proper bath. So she simply splashes water on her arms, legs and body. After Laraba fills her calabash, she leaves the stream. She wraps her long yellow and purple cloth around her body, twisting it together on her left side, just beneath her armpits. She balances the calabash on her head. Picking up her short-handled hoe, she continues the journey to her compound.

She wonders how many women from her village had come to the stream early this morning to wash their clothes. After doing their laundry, bathing, talking, singing and laughing together, she visualizes each placing her load of clothes on her head. They'd have taken them home to hang them on bushes to dry. Often she joins them, but today she wanted to work in her field.

An occasional trickle of cool water spills from the container. It runs down Laraba's neck and shoulders. This adds to the pleasure of her joyful thoughts of soon seeing her husband. She enjoys talking with him about the plants on her farm and their growth. She also shares the progress other women are making on their land around hers.

He tells about his trading and events in the market each day. It is restful to return home at the end of a busy day.

Suddenly visions of home vanish. Laraba pauses, gripped in pain. She clutches a small tree. She turns her head from side to side. Now the droplets running down her face aren't from the calabash on her head. Finally the discomfort subsides. She is able to walk on. It isn't long before she stops again, assaulted by another pain. Several times this slows her progress, but at last the village comes into view. She sees the stalked fence surrounding their family compound. She thinks, *just a little further. Will be in my compound.*

Laraba hurries to reach home. Walking through the entrance hut, she stoops so the water container won't strike the top of the low, roughly-hewn wooden door frame. After pouring water into the large clay pot near the cooking area, she puts her hoe in its place in her hut. Laraba looks about the compound to discover who is here. She is pleased the women in her family haven't returned from their fields or the market. She's glad the children are playing with neighbors elsewhere.

Before long Audu, tired and hungry, will be home from the market. Her heart pounds joyfully as she thinks about him. She loves him dearly!

As a child Audu had fallen on some rocks. He had broken off part of a tooth on the upper left side of his mouth. This and the slanted tribal marks on his face gave him a slightly crooked smile. He is about 5 feet 6 inches tall. That's the average height for men in his village. He's strong and manly with a lighter brown complexion than many of his people. Some people call him "that yellow man." His temper is quickly subdued. His bearing is composed and calm. Laraba loves him for being thoughtful of the feelings of others. He's resolute in manner to the point of daring, yet gentle and always fair and considerate.

"Uwa, are you here?" Laraba calls out, looking toward her mother-in-law's hut. There's no answer.

Immediately she goes to the cooking area to begin the preparation of their evening meal. This hut's roof is held high by four strong poles, one at each corner. There are no walls to catch the smoke from the fire under the family cooking pot. It sits on top of three large stones above a hole in the ground. With a fat fiber ball made from the residue left over after extracting the oil from the palm kernels, she kindles the fire. The aroma from many fires and hot red peppers used in their soup reminds Laraba that she is hungry. She must add more okra, tomatoes, and yam leaves to the soup tonight.

Laraba carefully watches to be sure that none of the flying sparks land aglow on the dry grass roofs. Little can cause greater concern than the smell of burning grass when the rains are few. She remembers seeing huts with their skeletons of stick and thatch burned away—the charred remains of once-prized possessions burned beyond use.

Uwa returns from the bush with a large bundle of firewood on her head. She sees Laraba holding tight to one of the poles of the cooking shed. After a few moments' pause, Laraba returns to her preparation of the jollof rice and pepper soup which they will eat this evening. The appetizing aroma of the food bubbling in the pot is carried on the breeze.

Uwa approaches with a smile. She admires her daughter-in-law. She knows this night will be an important one for her son. Audu has talked of little else but his plans for his first son, who will do great deeds for his people.

Laraba pauses from stirring the pot and greets her mother-in-law. Uwa is an elderly woman. She's thin with stooped shoulders and graying hair. Laraba thinks she is too old for this kind of work. Her dark brown face is furrowed with age and tribal marks but often holds a smile, radiating love and concern.

"It is time?" Uwa questions, smiling knowingly at her daughter-in-law, as she drops the heavy load to the ground.

"Yes, it is time," answers Laraba in a whisper. She is hesitant to share the wonderful secret. The close association between birth and death is never far from mind. The death of a revered elderly one can be accepted only with the expectation of a rebirth. Birth, life, death and birth: this cycle endlessly repeats itself. Who would return in the person of her child? Circumstances of the birth and facial features of the newborn should make it easy for the family, as well as the villagers, to know. Many times during her pregnancy Laraba has wondered who would be reincarnated in her baby. Now the time has come. She isn't sure she wants to talk about the birth.

"Audu will be happy. We will all be happy. The coming of a new one, a fresh voice, will bring joy to our compound," says Uwa.

Although Laraba doesn't answer, her smile appears brighter. Her eyes sparkle with a greater radiance. Just then, they hear Audu approaching.

"Let us wait until he has rested and taken food before we tell him," suggests Laraba.

"Yes, that will be good," agrees Uwa.

Laraba sits down on a three-legged stool and looks around at the compound. This has been her home for over four years. There are several huts made of mud and straw, each with its own purpose. Audu's father, Bako, built his compound like many others in this village. The thick walls topped with thatched grass roofs make them cooler in the hot weather than those that are now being built using tin for their roofs. The structures are all similar to each other. They vary only in size. Each of Bako's wives has her own hut. Her children live with her. But the hut of Bako's third wife, who died in childbirth, is now only a mound of dirt.

Toward the back of the yard is a small enclosed, unroofed area used as the latrine. A stunted, aged tree stands in the middle of the yard where several scrawny chickens and a thin dog often seek its shade.

The stalk fence surrounding their compound stops at the entrance hut. It's a cool room where visitors are welcomed and entertained. A fire in the center of the hut warms it during the cooler weather. This is when the harmattan, that bothersome dust-laden wind from the Sahara, is heavy and covers everything it touches with a red coating. Two large but short, smooth tree trunks facing each other serve as benches. When they don't provide enough room, woven grass mats are placed on the ground giving additional seats. If a special visitor of prominence comes, a chair is brought from inside the compound.

Each year during the last rains or soon after they are finished, mud is brought to repair the huts eroded by the downpours of water. If termites don't invade the grass roofs, they will last several years. But everyone knows that when those visitors do their work or when the grass becomes dark and rotten, it must be torn away. The building is re-roofed. If the sticks that support the grass are still adequate, they do not have to be replaced.

When Laraba first came, the oldest useable hut in the group was Bako's. Around his inside walls were many small compartments, like those in a pigeon-hole desk. These served as storage bins. Built out from the wall was a raised mud platform for sleeping. Underneath was a place for a small fire that made sleeping more comfortable during the cool season. However, the smoke reduced visibility and provoked sporadic coughing. The walls bear a blackness from the smoke of many fires. It's been a long time since a glowing fire had released its smoke, yet the smell of the last one still clings to the hut. Bako was buried inside. Now it serves as a store-house and is no longer used for sleeping.

Audu cycles into the compound with a package on his head. Placing his bicycle carefully against the tree, he speaks, "Business was good today. It was a good market."

Walking over to the cooking area, he continues, "Cloth for you and my son," as he hands Laraba the package.

She smiles as she catches the eyes of Uwa. "Cloth, again? Already you have bought enough to clothe the boy until he goes to school. He will be the best-dressed boy in the village with colors of red, green, and blue." Opening the package, she exclaimed, "It is beautiful!"

Her face radiates her deep affection for Audu. How often he shows his concern for her and the coming baby! Frequently he does that which is not expected in order to make her tasks easier.

"Rest now, for soon your food will be ready," she says.

As Audu smells the food cooking, his mouth waters in anticipation. He sits down on a low wooden stool near the cooking pot. When Laraba hands him his bowl, he starts eating without comment. Turning, he sees Laraba holding tight to her small stool.

"What is wrong? Are you sick?" he questions, speaking louder than he intended.

Laraba doesn't answer but soon releases her grip. Uwa turns and walks away from them into her own hut. When she's gone, Laraba goes over to stand behind Audu. She looks around the compound to see that no one is present. Then she places her hands on his shoulders. Lovingly she runs her fingers up his neck and holds his head. She leans over and whispers, "It is time."

Audu turns to look into Laraba's face. His eyes smile as he questions, "It is time? It is really time?" He watches her for a moment without speaking.

Presently his mother returns. Audu calls to her, "Uwa, it is time! It is time! We must prepare."

"Yes, I know. You rest. All will be done."

❖ ❖ ❖ ❖ ❖

The moon begins its journey across the African sky. The stars stand their watch as Uwa leads Laraba into her small round hut. Her mat, a box containing a few treasured items, a small lamp and a low stool are the primary articles in Laraba's hut. From time to time she cries out as the pains come more often. The perspiration, tears and sobbing don't make them easier.

Audu places more wood on the fire under the cooking pot. He thinks he will take food again later. He jumps with the sound of every cry. His body aches as the tension draws his muscles tight.

Backing away from the blaze, he reaches for the amulets hanging from his waist. They were designed and made by the local juju priest. Small leather pouches in different sizes are attached to a leather band. They contain various things like feathers, small stones, crooked teeth or bones. The waist band can be adjusted to fit the owner. Though he wears them constantly, he seldom gives any thought to them. Now he tightly grasps the amulets. They are needed to guard against evil and injury. Only when they chafe his hands does he release them to ease the irritation. He wonders how they can offer any protection, but he wouldn't have uttered this thought aloud. *Who would dare question?* He must do everything he can to pacify the gods. He wonders if Laraba prepared well for his son. *Did she seek the protection of enough amulets?*

Why do I have this feeling of concern? He sighs, thinking this will be a very long night. Often he had known fear, but this was like none he had ever experienced before.

As people hear the news, they come to join Audu in the waiting. He moves outside of his compound to be with them. But he remains where he can still hear the sounds from Laraba's hut.

All eyes suddenly focus on an old woman. She hobbles, supported by her stick, across the compound and enters Laraba's hut. Everyone knows Soho, the midwife; she has shared in many births. She knows their ways. Not only is she competent, but expects to be called to a birthing. She would be offended had she not been summoned. She comes now to do the job that is hers, and with her come two assistants. They are learning from her the profession that she has gained through much experience.

From a distance, a dog's bark pierces the air. Gradually others sound as though they too are joining in the vigil. The wind awakens and climbs among the trees, whistling quietly. Later, fruit bats begin their flight through the darkness. They search for food and adventure. They don't count the hazards of the night as others must.

The cries of pain and fear become louder and more frequent, and the crowd grows as the word spreads from compound to compound. In a village where little happens, the birth of a child brings excited crowds. As the people arrive, they seek a place to sit near Audu's compound. The women stay together beneath a small kapok tree to one side of the compound entrance hut. The men are beside another tree not far away. Under the blanket of twinkling stars, most of them are in animated conversations, but a few sit in silence. Someone begins singing a round of verses in a song. It's about the joy of having a child and what his life will be like. Others join in. New verses are added. Some of the women dance about, clapping their hands.

Slowly, the hours of the night drag by. Audu, deep in his own thoughts, knows now that Laraba will prove her worth. She will soon be the mother of a son. Perhaps in time there'll be more children, many sons and perhaps even a daughter. Yes, that would be all right, after his sons, a daughter. How pleased he was when Laraba told him she was with child! He knew she was a good worker and a pleasant companion. NOW she is fruitful as well. If a woman can bear children, many children, she is a prize to be coveted.

They had been married too long without having children. His family had begun pressing him to take another wife. There'd been talk of a young girl in a neighboring compound who wasn't betrothed. Though she wasn't yet capable of child bearing, her parents were discussing her desirability as a wife. Yes, he'd thought of taking another wife. Laraba was becoming self-supporting and would be able to support their children, if they had any. Another wife would soon be able to do the same. Perhaps one day, when he has acquired enough money to purchase one, he might take another wife. And eventually he'd have several wives. After all, that would allow his fellow villagers to consider him a wealthy man. But when Laraba finally became pregnant, he was satisfied with her.

Audu hadn't known her when she was brought to their compound. Then she was a shy, awkward girl. In time, he began to enjoy her company. It wasn't long before she became a favorite with his family. His father had chosen well. This night will be proof of that.

As Audu continues his musings, he visualizes Laraba. She is strikingly desirable. She is short and slender with small shoulders and large hips, good for child-bearing. Her enormous, bright brown eyes sparkle. Her even, white teeth often show in her broad, free smile behind full lips. Her dark face is smooth since she doesn't wear tribal marks. Now her abdomen is large and strained. Her smooth deep brown skin is drawn tight. Her curly hair, black and lustrous, shines in the sunlight.

Soon Laraba will deliver his son, which will be the fulfillment of many dreams. Audu thought of the good times he and his son would have. He'll laugh and play and grow. He must go to school. Not many in the village attend school, but already he planned for his son to attend classes. His son must complete school, not stop with Class IV as he had done. With education, life will be happier. He'll make much money and have all the things money can provide. Perhaps he'll have enough money to help their people when the crops fail or trading is poor. They'll hunt together. On and on his mind races through the plans and pleasures of life.

Suddenly, his attention is sharply brought back to the present as a cry, a different one, a weaker sound is heard. It is that of a new-born baby.

Audu springs to his feet and listens intently. There it is again! He smiles and laughs and claps his hands. He finds it hard to contain himself. He dances around the group of men. Others soon join in the celebration. A drummer begins beating out a rhythm designed to encourage dancing. Audu's son is born! The men and women in the crowd are laughing and talking, many anticipating the naming ceremony which will soon take place.

"I can hardly wait for the celebration and feasting," one man states.

"Yes, that will not be too long away," responds Audu, smiling. He is too happy and excited to think about that just now.

"What joy we will have eating, drinking, dancing, singing and drumming all day and all night for a week," a young man shares with enthusiasm.

Each thinks of the part he or she likes best. All know there'll be more excitement then than tonight. But this night gives birth to the other. The men agree among themselves that Audu is a fine man and Laraba is an adequate woman.

The women are busy sharing with each other Laraba's value. "The events of this night prove Laraba is a good wife," states one of the women.

"She will make a good mother too."

"Yes, she has shown love for the children in our village. So she will love her own," continues the admiration, voiced by yet another.

A young woman speaks loudly. "She works diligently on her farm and raises delicious maize."

"She respects her husband and his family also," chimes in an older woman.

"All fine qualities in Laraba!" concludes a shy woman sitting on the side.

CHAPTER TWO

Horror Replaces Joy

Another cry—loud and painful—then a weaker sound, the cry of another newborn! SILENCE!!

The old woman, Soho, moves quickly from the hut and hastens out of the compound. She is followed by her assistants. She doesn't speak. The midwife steals through their midst. The bewildered people make way for her as she slips by. The waiting, watching crowd murmurs. All are caught in fear. What has happened? Is there cause for concern?

Audu runs into the hut. A small, flickering lamp projects grotesque patterns on the walls. Sitting on the floor is Laraba. She is pressed against the mud wall. Her hands cover her face. She is shaking. Deep sobs escape her lips.

Uwa sits on a low stool, staring blankly at nothing. Fear and confusion permeate the room.

"It is a bad night. Evil is here," Uwa whispers in anguish. Her voice breaks. Hot tears run down her cheeks.

Audu stops. He looks at the baby. But he sees not one, but two. "Aee-ee-ee, oh, no, no!" he cries, "Oh, why? Oh, why? OH, WHY?"

He looks again. Must be sure. He really does see two. He screams, "IT CANNOT BE!!"

He trembles at what he sees. All of his life he's heard that the birth of two brings misfortune, trouble, and heartache. He is dazed. He feels ill. Agony engulfs the small dark hut. He is horrified by the silence. Gasping for breath, Audu feels he is being smothered. Without thought or any words, he lifts the cloth upon which one twin had been dropped on the other. His arms are filled with evil. His only thought is that he must remove this curse. He leaves the gloomy hut of despair with his bundle of shame.

In silent desperation, Uwa watches Audu leave. In her exhausted and shocked condition, Laraba hardly notices what is happening. Then she collapses on her mat.

This new father hurries out of his compound and stumbles through the crowd. They shrink from him. In stunned silence, the people look at each other with questioning eyes. Swiftly, they leave their places of observation.

Audu picks up his pace. Quickly, his dreams have been shattered. Plans vanished. They are replaced by fear and uncertainty. He must get rid of this curse. It can't be allowed to stay in his compound. The load is light. Even so, his back and shoulders ache.

"But—why?? Why??" he questions. "This night should have been filled with joy. But it has turned into a horrible tragedy!" he moans, as he leaves his village.

Audu starts in the direction of the stream, which is some distance away. He thinks he'll place them there. He could let them drown and leave them to float off. People have done that.

The babies begin crying. This doesn't slow him down. He has to get rid of these wicked creatures.

About halfway to the stream, he changes his mind. He decides instead to go to the forbidden forest. In the past he had avoided that dreadful place—that burial ground. No one goes there by choice. He shudders at the thought, but deliberately moves forward. That's the place for them. It's where lepers, those who committed suicide, and those who died of contagious diseases are taken.

❖ ❖ ❖ ❖ ❖

After Audu left, Uwa picks up the placentas. She leaves the hut walking with a dull, unsteady gait. As she goes outside, a restless moving cloud silently shrouds the moon. A cool breeze touches her shoulders. She shivers. The matter is placed on the ground. Going to her own hut, she gets her hoe. She buries the afterbirth. Usually this is the work of the mother. But, in her despair, Laraba couldn't be expected to perform this tedious task.

Soon Uwa realizes that Audu hadn't carried a large pot in which to place the twins. Had he taken a hoe or digger to make a grave? Uwa frets as she thinks of him—alone, carving out a place for the two far from home. Rarely is one buried away from the family compound. There'll be no mourners at this burial. No funeral oration. No drumming. No drinking. No dancing after the last thud of earth had stilled. The young male goat Audu had purchased for a sacrifice to the gods won't spill its blood as a thanks offering. There'll be no feasting on the roasted meat.

"Aiee! Oh! My son!" she wails.

Uwa begins to think about birth, life and death. She wonders if their birth and death matter. She felt it did for one. But with two? She had seen the sadness brought by twins in the lives of others. But it had no meaning for her. Now it is close and personal. These are her grandchildren. However, nothing more can be done. There'll be no planning. No hope. No dreams for the future of a cherished grandchild. Never had the possibility of this burden entered her mind when her own children were born.

Bako, her husband, had never mentioned it either, though it had happened to his third wife. She had twins, and they had been destroyed. Still, she died. Yet Uwa and Bako had never talked about this. Nevertheless, the procedure was clear. The evil resulting from twins wasn't often discussed. But it had been done frequently enough for all to know what must be done. A few experiences like this one keeps the villagers reminded. There are terrible results. Action must be taken.

Uwa's face mirrors her haggard spirit. Beads of perspiration hang on her forehead. She can't control the tremor of her hands. Bako's other wives and their children quietly slipped into their own huts. They speak in whispers about what has happened. They question what will happen to their family. This leaves Uwa alone. She feels the need to talk, but there's no one here. This is an experience unknown to her. Seldom has she needed anyone. Not often has she been alone. Now she is desperate. If only there were someone to hear her expression of the grief. Then perhaps her trembling could be controlled. Again, she begins to cry. She is unable to control her sorrow and confusion. She doesn't want to control them.

Almost under her breath, she mumbles, "Why has this happened? Why?"

Uwa staggers into the dark black shadows of the compound. Realizing that she still holds the hoe, she lets it drop. In her anguish, she doesn't hear the full sound as it strikes the ground. She braces herself against the cool wall of her hut. Tears stream down her face. In the past these had not come easily.

She hasn't frequently visited the sacred tree. Uwa wonders what more visits there would have accomplished. Would another amulet around Laraba's waist have kept this evil away? Distraught, she remembers that she failed to call on the juju priest often. With so much to do, it hadn't seemed necessary. But, was it?

◆　◆　◆　◆　◆

Warm dust covers Audu's feet as he passes though the plots of guinea corn. The wind runs through the long leaves and bends the heads of the sorghum until they touch. As he approaches another stream, the smell of cows—a pleasant aroma for a farmer—catches his attention. The friendly herdsmen with their brahmans are nearby. The cattle are followed by the white laki-laki birds. These people were always good for a story or conversation. Now they are sleeping in their crudely-constructed temporary stalk huts, unaware of the tragedy of this night.

The trail crosses through a body of water. Usually, he quickened his pace when he approached it because of the enjoyment awaiting him; the water soothed his feet. But tonight he gives only a moment's notice to this pleasure. His feet are heavy. His task is grave.

He begins his climb up the knoll and into the bush. The babies cry again. Audu shuts out the sounds of their tiny voices. He thinks about the wild animals he might meet as they roam the forest. He almost loses his balance several times on the uneven dirt path. Once, he stumbles on a protruding stone and falls to his knees. The babies make it difficult for him to get to his feet. He places them on the ground until he can stand. Picking them up, he decides to make his strides shorter. Every step is an extreme effort as he moves in the moonlight through the tangled bush. The trail is rough and difficult to follow. He can't see very well. Going in the wrong direction when the path seems to divide, he gets lost.

Before long, Audu comes to a large rock that is in his way. He can't step over it. The growth is too thick to go around it. Turning around, he slowly goes back. He finds the path. He shuffles along farther. He begins to sense that he is approaching the forbidden forest. Finally he stops.

"This must be the place," he whispers. He lays his burden down at the base of a large tree. Audu doesn't look at them. He can't. "This is the way it must be. This is the way it has always been," he assures himself. The terrible task he has appointed to himself is wearily completed.

Audu is tormented by the silence and his grief. He slowly starts the arduous journey back to his hut. He questions what evil the two might carry. He knows he has done this to protect his family. Destroying them will avenge the gods and divert their attention elsewhere.

His grief isn't for those he has left in the forbidden bush. It is for himself and Laraba. Sorrow swells through his terror. *What will he do now? Who is to blame?* Suddenly, he gulps. He remembers what he had seen in the jungle only yesterday when he had visited a nearby village market. The red monkeys! At the time he gave no thought to them. Now he remembers the stories he has heard about dead twins continuing life in the form of these monkeys. He wonders if the red monkeys had been a warning.

CHAPTER THREE

Grandma's Grief

Uwa can't sleep until Audu returns. She sits alone outside on her stool groaning. She ponders what could have caused this awful thing. What will be the results for everyone? She remembers seeing Yahaya, the juju priest's son, a few days earlier. He had sneered, saying, "So you think you will be a grandmother?" Uwa questions whether his father had warned him about what was coming.

Looking about at the shadows of the compound, she thinks about her life. Her face is twisted with her grief. Her thoughts aren't only of this night. She considers her days and years as a wife and mother. She was Bako's first wife. As the head wife, it was her duty to help each new wife find her place and her responsibilities in the compound. Uwa learned to settle disputes among the family members. She gained respect for her abilities as a leader. Now she feels they have all left her to suffer alone.

Her thoughts turn to her own children. Talata, her oldest daughter, has been married three years to a polygamist. He has seven other wives. Still, she doesn't have a child of her own. There are rumors she will be sent home. She causes squabbles in her husband's house. Often she is the subject of gossip among the other wives in the compound. When she visited last year, she argued constantly with others in the compound. Talata was taunted by the women of the village for being barren and unkempt. In fact, she didn't have her hair plaited even once during the month she was here. The need was evident when she arrived. She left trash and pots scattered around the courtyard for someone else to clean up. Even as a child, she failed to do her share of the work. She gives little attention to anything. Uwa wonders why she is like this.

And Riti, her second daughter, married for several years already, doesn't yet have a child. Perhaps this will be the year. Riti was always interested in men. She was given in marriage early. Though she isn't as nice looking as the other girls, her husband seems pleased with her. She is well liked and will be a good mother.

Bala, the oldest son is Uwa's pride. He's away at school. He's not married, but she knows he will do well in life. He was one of the best students in his classes in his primary and secondary schools. He always came home neat and clean. He walks straight and tall.

A smile crosses her lips as she thinks of Bala. She feels he is a fine man. He'll have many children when the time comes. Surely he'll soon be interested in marriage. He is past the usual age to marry. She knows she needs to talk more strongly to him the next time he comes home. If only her husband Bako still lived, he would have already made arrangement for marriage. He'd have seen to it. Now Uwa must depend on Bako's brother for this guidance. He's not as interested as a father. A father places his son's needs above his own.

She sighs heavily and wraps her arms tightly around her knees as she sits quietly. Thoughts of Uwa's youngest daughter creep into her mind. Roda sweeps her hut regularly. She always sees that her clothes are clean. She seems to like to do any job given to her. She doesn't fuss about going out early in the morning to take the goats to feed. She's still too young for marriage and children. In time she will have many children. Even now a man in a nearby village is showing an interest in marrying her. With grandchildren Uwa will be a proper grand-mother! But Audu was to have fulfilled her dream.

She shakes her head in anguish, remembering when Laraba was brought to her compound. She came as Audu's wife. Laughter and joy came with her. Without question, she accepts the work given her. Seldom does she complain. Even when the sun beats down upon her back and the hot heavy air filled with dust causes her lips to be dry and cracked, she can smile. She works hard to prevent the mold from growing in the dark huts after the rain comes.

Before Laraba became pregnant, Uwa had started urging Audu to seek another wife. She wanted him to have children. Upon learning of Laraba's pregnancy, Uwa was happy. She wished Bako were alive. He would've been pleased. He had chosen Laraba for Audu. When Laraba was very young Bako often visited Jato, her father. Well did Uwa remember the day Bako returned with the news.

"It is agreed," he said with a smile. He recounted every detail of the conversation he had with Jato. It was over the payment of the bride price. Their friendly exchange of views brought both men pleasure.

"Good, I am glad. Laraba will make Audu a faithful and acceptable wife," Uwa remembers saying.

Bako lived only a few months after Laraba came to their compound as Audu's bride. His new daughter-in-law helped make those months happy times. She prepared his favorite soup, rich with bits of meat, palm oil, peppers, bitter leaves, okra, tomatoes, and spices. Often Laraba took time to talk with him. This meant she mostly listened to his long stories.

One of his favorite tales was about the greedy hyena who found some meat. He was happy. It was getting dark when he came to a river. He saw the reflection of himself in the water and thought that hyena's meat was bigger than his own. As he reached in to grab it away from the other one's mouth, he lost his own meat. When Bako told this to Laraba, he would throw back his head and laugh. Then he added that seeing and wanting so badly can cause you trouble.

He also enjoyed talking about African proverbs. "One is better than none," was one he explained to her. It is better to be satisfied with what you have than to want something more or different. "God makes it so," was another one he liked. She learned many interesting and helpful things from Bako.

Uwa's attention returns to the present as she hears a goat begging to be released. It's in a stable that stands in one corner of the compound. Soon Roda will take it and its companions out to feed. That building is as well-cared for as are those of the family. The floor is slightly slanted to allow water to run off and out the back. As with most of the other huts, the floor is made of cow dung mixed with mud, making a hard smooth surface that is easy to keep clean and discourages insects from living there.

Not far away, built upon several rocks, are smaller, conical mud granaries for guinea corn and millet. A large opening is in the top of each where the grain can be poured in. After the granaries are filled, the top openings are capped with thatched roofs. They are constructed with small openings near the bottom where the grain can be removed. Those openings are also closed to prevent bush rats and other small animals from entering. Clean, cooled ashes from the cooking fires are added to the grain from time to time to deter insects. In this compound, there are two such granaries.

Uwa often felt proud of her husband. Bako was a good provider. He enjoyed telling stories about his family and loved children. He liked to watch them play their games. He also licked his lips with pleasure after a delicious meal. Now she misses many things about him.

"Oh, how I miss you," she speaks to the shadows. But her thoughts return to the present.

In the last few months, she has enjoyed imagining the future. She knew Audu and Laraba would be good parents. They would teach the child all he needed to know to live successfully here in their village.

In her mind's eye, she watched as her young grandchild grew. Uwa could almost feel him on her back as she worked in her compound. If he became unhappy, she would sway side-to-side. That would put him to sleep, lying against her body warm and secure. She could imagine seeing him sit at the edge of the circle of men, listening as they talked. He would learn about the past and hear them discuss the future. Or he would run to the farm to help until he was big enough to learn the work of a man. She planned to teach him to bring water and firewood. Beginning with a small empty bucket or a gourd, he would balance it on his head. The container would then be only partly filled. He would continue his training until at last he developed a strong neck capable of balancing and carrying a heavy load. He'd also sit with her in the market and learn to trade.

Pleasant visions had raced through her mind as she watched Laraba at her work. Soon, she'd be able to sit with the other village grandmothers and be proud. She had been snubbed by those who had grandchildren. Bako's other wives mocked her as they bragged about their own. Some women laughed at her in the market because Audu didn't marry another woman who could bear children. But she had planned to bear this blessing with dignity. She might strut a bit, but she'd be careful not to offend. Now her dreams are crushed. It seems forever since she had had those thoughts.

Yet, just yesterday her excitement of the expected birth filled her imagination. Now it seemed an eternity ago. In its place, she anticipates evil filling their compound.

Because all the excited, interested villagers of the earlier evening are gone, an eerie silence fills the night. This is accented by frightening shadows created by the dying, flickering firelight. Uwa looks about at those shadows in anxiety and wonders what evil they hold. Everyone in her compound is afraid. The entire village feels the presence of the great curse that came in the night to the compound of Audu. Every house is filled with questions. Each person is suspicious of Laraba and Audu. Many are asking, "What wicked thing has Laraba done? What evil has Audu committed? Why has misfortune overtaken them? What will happen to all of us?"

In the moonlight, Uwa sees Audu enter the compound. She wants to talk with him but decides against it. Instead, she leaves him to his grief. She feels her way around the hut to her door. Entering, she finds her mat. She unrolls it and tries to go to sleep. That will be a long time coming.

◆ ◆ ◆ ◆ ◆

The moon is finishing its course and the swarm of stars are leaving their places. But Audu doesn't notice the sky or anything else as he drags himself into his compound. He doesn't see Uwa sitting near the dying fire.

He enters the hut which he built a few months ago when he had been considering taking another wife. Besides, Laraba is unclean. He'll not go to be with her now. Many thoughts and many questions claim Audu's mind as he lies down on his sleeping mat. He thinks he should have put the babies in the river. He ponders why he wasn't able to do that. Now, what evil can he expect to attack his family?

He's exhausted. But it's almost daylight before fretful sleep comes. He hears neither the crowing of the cocks in the early morning nor the rain that comes suddenly and dances on the tin roofs in the distance.

CHAPTER FOUR

A Flight Begins

Sometime in the night, Laraba suddenly awakens, startled. Pain and panic keep her from rising. *Terrible nightmare. Could not have happened. My legs will not move. Am I glued to my sleeping mat?* Fretting as she lies there, she gradually realizes it wasn't a dream. It is real. She begins to remember—*two babies? What happened? Why? What did I do to cause this evil thing? What could I have done to prevent it?* Question after question races through her mind. *What suffering will this birth of two bring to me? Our family? Our village? What will we do now?* Her mind is jammed with so many concerns and anxious thoughts that she can't sort out.

She remembers many stories about alarming things happening that were blamed on such births. Her apprehension grows as she remembers the time when the chief's daughter gave birth to twins. She died. Did the two cause their mother's death? Then a fire destroyed the chief's compound. His own mother died in the blaze. Her death was explained by the delay in destroying the two. How could such a thing be? She tosses upon her mat.

As she recalls events after the birth of twins, she wonders if they are the children of a certain kind of fairy. That's what some people say. If so, do they return and bring trouble? She laments that perhaps they do bring difficulties. She thinks about another time when two babies were born to the same woman. It is true that for a long time afterwards the villagers noted how poor the farm crops were. Greedy grasshoppers had devoured their corn and yams, leaving only stalks stripped of their leaves and produce. Rain had come sparingly. The entire village had suffered from hunger. Young children's bellies became distended.

Laraba's expected joy is choked by the grief brought on by the birth of two. Evil saturates everything when two are born. As a child she had heard the women talk of the trouble multiple births brought.

She clearly remembers her mother saying, "Twins are dangerous. They must be destroyed. That will drive the evil away. The power of two will be eliminated."

In the past, she'd given silent assent to these beliefs. Now, secretively in her heart she asked why? *Why? WHY?* Her people had known other hardships. There were no twins to cause those difficulties. What had been the cause of the trouble then?

My babies! I yearn to hold their tiny warm bodies against my breast. The softness of the first overwhelmed me with excitement. Joy and happiness were in my hut. Suddenly a change. The birth of the second child brought panic and fear. Immediately all those gathered in the hut with Laraba, except Uwa, were gone. How fast they had fled! Just as quickly the babies were gone. In swift succession she thinks, *where are my babies? Must find them. Go against the ways of my people? Be an outcast. As a woman, can I venture out to look for them?*

Again, in her mind she hears their cries. She imagines how it would feel to hold them. *Will do whatever it takes to find them and keep them.* Regardless of the customs and pressures of her people, Laraba knows she must find her babies. Her mind struggles with many possibilities.

Return to my people with twins? Trade my family for my babies? How will we live? Have little money. It will soon be gone. Where can we go? Where are my babies? They must be cold and hungry. They need me. I need them. I want them. I will find them. I am their mother. I must go now and find them.

Laboring to breathe, she struggles to get up from her mat. She shivers as she thinks about the risks she is taking. Yet she is sure what she'll do. She crawls around the circular hut until she finds her small lamp. Quietly, she lights it with a match stuck upside down in the dirt at the edge of her floor. Laraba stands and steadies herself against the wall. In the dim light, she finds her box. She binds her body with some soft white cloth. With tears streaming down her cheeks, she pushes aside the bright material Audu had brought from the market only the day before. Instead, she selects several long, rectangular pieces of dark cloth. These are used as wrappers or skirts. She also takes out some slightly smaller matching strips she'll need to tie the babies on her back. Some dark head ties, a couple of blouses, a sleeveless dress and a cotton slip are put on top of the pile. Except for the things she'll wear, she folds the other things and wraps them in one of the larger piece of material she had laid on the floor.

This bundle she'll carry on her head when she leaves. Her fingers go to her throat and ears. She touches her reddish-yellow gold necklaces and earrings that match. She decides to wear them. But she'll leave the heavy coral jewelry. With trembling hands, she takes all of the notes and coins she had saved from the sale of her maize last year. She ties them in the end of a long, narrow cloth. This is placed around her waist under her body cloth. The money was intended to pay her baby's school fees, but now there is a more pressing need.

Though weak and numb, she rolls up her sleeping mat and places it against the wall. Feeling a little dizzy, she leans against the wall a moment, then slips quietly out of her hut.

She dares not enter the larger part of the compound to secure food to take with her. She glances around, then leaves. Her drawn face shows her despair as she glances back to view her home—seeing its outline for the last time.

She turns away to steal through the shadows. Laraba's aware of the slightest sound. She covers her mouth with her hands to shut in the gasps she feels in her heart. Shaking her head, she mouths without a sound, "What am I doing?"

Although she realizes Audu was doing her job of destroying the babies, Laraba feels sure he couldn't do all that is required concerning the babies. She must find them quickly. Never had she dreamed of such a journey. Nothing must stop her now. Silently, she sneaks through the sleeping village. Every few minutes she looks back over her shoulder to be sure she isn't being followed. Her heart's pounding so fast she feels she might faint. But there isn't a moment to waste.

She shrinks from angry voices and hides in the darkness. Every nerve and muscle in her body is taut. Only inches away from her, arguing comes from behind the closed tin door of a hut. The man and woman don't hear her. Right now they aren't the least interested in her problems. They have difficulties of their own—too little money, too many demands, and little confidence in or love for each other. The couple faces the trials of life together as best they can.

The path she follows at this point is narrow. The houses almost touch each other. As she weaves her way through the maze of huts, she slips on some water. It is running from under one of the mud walls. She feels the oozing mud cover her feet, but hurries on. Somewhere, hidden from sight, a rooster announces the approaching dawn.

"My hoe! If only I had brought my hoe. It would serve me well now. That would stop many questions. One doesn't go to the farm without it or a cutlass," she murmurs softly.

Laraba clutches her body cloths closer against the sharp morning air. She tries to go faster as the daylight begins to appear. When she reaches the grass near the first farm, she trips and falls. This startles a covey of bush fowl that explode in flight before her. She has disturbed the birds on their way to a farm for feeding. Laraba's so nervous that her heart almost stops beating for a moment. Struggling to rise from the grass, she realizes she has cut her hand as she braced herself against the fall. The need to stop and rest almost overpowers her, but her heart cries within her. *My babies. Must find them. They need me, and oh, how I want them!*

At a nearby stream, Laraba looks to see if the babies are in the water. They aren't here. She stops the bleeding of her hand and gets a drink of water. Then she presses on in her search. She shakes her head and moans softly. She ponders how difficult her task is. *How will I ever find them? Where did Audu go with them?* She sighs. *So tired, but must keep looking until I have them in my arms.*

Laraba drags herself from one place to another—looking, listening. She searches around the trees and under heavy bushes along the path. She goes to the stream. Only yesterday, she splashed in the water, got a drink and filled her calabash here. She thinks Audu might have left the babies in this body of water. When she doesn't find them, she moves away. She quickens her steps. The warmth of the hot tropical sun bears down upon her. *I have got to find my little ones soon. Their soft, tender skin cannot endure burning from the sun. Other dangers crowd her troubled mind. What if an animal or a snake finds the babies and devours them? What if some person discovers them? What if a heavy rain comes?* "Do not think about things like that," she tells herself. Then she remembers her village.

She speaks aloud without even realizing it. "What must the villagers be thinking now? Have I been missed? Are they even now looking for me?" Reaching up, she holds her head between her hands, as she groans, "What is to become of us?"

Heavy concerns fill her mind. *Have to stay away from places where anyone might see me. All know of the curse brought by twins. But I must find my babies.*

Moving around a thick growth surrounding some thorn trees, she comes to a ravine. "I do not remember this place," she mouths softly. "Have I ever been here before? Maybe I do not want to remember it."

Following the path the water had worn, she picks her way through the large gully. Between two granite rocks, she watches a mother scorpion and her young consume a large insect. Laraba steps more carefully among the rocks to avoid the dangerous sting of such ugly creatures.

Whenever any sound pierces the stillness, she pauses to catch a cry in the distance. Recognizing the sound as that of a bird or an animal, she forces herself to keep going. Farther into the woods, it's deep and still and eerie. Birds and animals are silent as though they too are afraid. The thick, dark jungle is as impenetrable as her own actions. She can't tell why this terrible tragedy has occurred. Nor does she know why she is searching for the twins. What she is doing is against all that she has been taught by her elders. But this doesn't matter to her now.

There's little breeze in the thick bush. The stifling heat surrounds and holds her tightly. She can hardly breathe. The gray branches and green leaves have interlaced to make a canopy almost as closely woven as the thatched roof of her hut. Still, the heat reaches the undergrowth. Aching in mind and body, Laraba shuffles on. Often she reaches up to steady the load on her head.

"Will I find them in time?" she moans aloud to herself. She can think of nothing but rescuing her little ones.

The sun's rays cast irregular shadows on the ground wherever they penetrate the thickness. She trudges on through the quietness. Her senses are keen to every movement. Even though she doesn't see them, she is conscious of several birds here and there fluttering from tree limb to tree limb. With each passing moment, her uneasiness grows. She can't stop the passing of time or calm her troubled mind. Perspiration trickles down her face and body. Even in the deep shadows, the power of the sun soaks her body. Her mind races on. The anxiety is almost unbearable. Her head throbs. She twists her hands against each other and rubs her arms with her tired hands.

"Where? Oh, where could Audu have taken them?" Laraba questions. *If only Audu and I had spoken about this. But we did not. Must keep on searching.*

The sun is directly over her head. Her legs ache and her knees are weak. Keeping her back straight seems impossible. Knots fill her stomach. Unsteady hands grab her dry throat and quivering lips. The load falls from her head. She sinks to the ground under an umbrella tree to rest. *If I find my babies, how can it be all right to keep them? What if I cannot find them?* She questions whether or not she has the strength or will to continue her search. She puts her head in her hands and sobs.

As she relaxes, her babies' plight returns to her mind. Regaining her motivation, she strains to stand and haltingly walks on. The cover of trees and bush gives way to rocky, barren ground. Suddenly she finds herself in full daylight and a bleak terrain. The stark landscape increases her anxiety. She isn't welcome in this place.

"The twins are not here," she whispers. "Surely Audu would not have stopped and placed them on open ground."

With a burst of new hope, she returns to the trees and thick growth. "If I am to find them, it will be in the bush," she cautions herself.

Laraba stops abruptly. There is a strange noise in the bush beside her. *What is it?* Her heart beats frantically. She holds her breath. From its hiding place of comfort and security, a rabbit hops across her path. The furry one hadn't seen nor heard her. She remains rooted in the spot as the small animal goes on its way. *That rabbit knows better where it is going than I do.*

Pausing a moment, she pulls her cloth from the fingers of a sharp bush that had snagged it. She works carefully to release it, but her hands are torn in the effort to free herself. Again she thinks of her babies' tender skin, so soft and new.

"Oh, I need to find them and hold them," she cries out to the silent bush.

The brush in front of her is so thick she can't pass through it. Turning to the left she finds her way. Laraba's steps falter. She's hungry. She's lonely. Just then, a large brown lizard with an orange head scurries from the grass across her path. Another darts after it. As she looks into the bush where the two went, she realizes that no one is ever completely alone.

Her physical discomfort ravages her mind. *Am tired and thirsty. But, how hungry and thirsty must my little ones be. No rest until I find them. Nothing else matters.*

"There is still time. I know I will find them. Even now I feel I am near them," she mutters an encouraging word to herself.

She trudges on, peering into the bush, always listening intently to every sound. She strains her ears, hoping to hear a cry—the cry of her own. But there is only silence.

After hours of wandering, Laraba discovers she's returned to the ravine. Reaching to catch an overhanging limb, she lifts herself up. She sees them. They are circling high in the afternoon sky. Three vultures hover in the upper air. What is their carrion? Her heart stands still. Those buzzards grow larger as they descend lower and lower. She trembles as she thinks about their prey. Her spirit plunges to a new low.

"Ai-e-e! Ai-e-e-e!" she cries in anguish. She moves anxiously toward them. The large birds are landing. They've been drawn to the smell and taste of death. She stumbles and falls. Her head load tumbles to the ground. It is left there. Unable to rise she crawls on the rocky ground. Soon her knees are bleeding. Cringing, she slowly goes on.

"My babies!"

Approaching a foul odor, she clutches a small acacia tree. Laraba struggles to get up. Looking around, she discovers the bird's dinner on the ground.

How had it begun? There she sees—in a place made clear by the thrashing of its wings. A large bird had died in a forgotten trap. Several of the vultures scatter into the air as Laraba approaches. She has interrupted their feast. One determined creature continues to tear at the putrefying flesh of the trapped bird. Finally, even that predator rises swiftly into the sky. It carries in its beak a piece of flesh ripped from his prey. Laraba is gripped by nausea from the odor and the sight of the dead bird. She grasps her nose to keep out the stench. Relief washes over her because it is not her children the vultures seek. Eager to leave this place of death, she creeps away. She picks up her clothes and goes on.

"I must find my little ones safe," she screams, though no one hears her plea.

As she leaves the area, she cringes at what she has seen. *What kind of person would leave a trap untended like that? How many days had the trapper eagerly worked his traps only to find them empty? Why did he not come today? Surely he would have come if he could.* Unexpected thoughts occur to Laraba. *Life is like that trap and must be tended every day. Failure on any given day at any given moment can bring meaningless tragedy. People can dream, but they must not forget their responsibilities.*

What has Audu done with our babies? Has he returned home? Is he even now in our compound? Have to stop thinking about him. Must find our children.

Near panic, she moves out into an opening. She sees a small farm. On the other side are several footpaths. Which way should I go? Looking up into the clear sky, she receives no indication about which direction she should take. Instinct drives her to take the middle path. Before long she enters another farm.

"Where am I?" Laraba wails aloud.

The ripe guinea corn towers above her. Its sharp leaves cut at her arms and legs. She hears the sound of tiny feet running away. The plants sway slightly. Several rats have scampered away, frightened by her coming. *I made you afraid, so you left your ordinary way of finding food. Just so, because I am afraid, I have left my routine. But I must hasten to find my babies.*

"Life is one fear after another." She agonizes. "Why must it always be so?"

Laraba remembers that it's the big market day of the week. Few, if any, will be at their farms. So she is no longer afraid of being seen. *Am far from my own farm. Stay away from the main roads and busy footpaths. Should not meet anyone along the way.* Her thoughts again turn to Audu. *Where could he have taken the two? Is he still carrying them? Has he taken them to the river? There was a mother who held her two under the water until they stopped breathing. That would be the easiest way. Could Audu do such a thing?* She sighs. Tears stream down her face.

"Oh, I hope not," she breathes through clenched teeth. She shakes her head as she speaks to herself, "I do not believe he could do that. He is too kind and gentle."

Again, she longs to sit a few minutes under the shadow of a large neem tree that stands a few feet away, but she must keep moving. If she stops, she might not be able to get to her feet again. She continues to ponder the stream. She feels an urge to return to it. *What if Audu is there with the babies? What will he do? What can I say? What would happen?*

A thought abruptly enters her mind. *Would Audu take them to the forbidden bush? Have always stayed away from that place. People don't go there except to bury the dead who must be abolished from the living because of their evil. Who can tell what might happen to someone who dares to approach the forbidden forest? Evil is always lurking around, ready to harm or destroy. Should I, a woman, dare approach that place?* She shivers as she recounts some of the stories she has heard about that miserable place. *Surely Audu would not take them there. Am deathly afraid to go there—I WILL go. The forbidden bush is toward the rising sun from my village.*

Looking at the sun, Laraba decides which direction to travel. Slowly, she staggers that way. The agitation in her heart fills her stomach with pain. It dulls her dark eyes. Shadows lengthen. She mustn't be in the forbidden bush after dark. She trudges along the narrow trail. It begins to rain. She lifts one hand to steady the load on her head, but soon she has to stop under another tree for protection. She leans against the trunk. Her weary eyes need rest. She closes them against the downpour of water. Finally, the rain stops. She proceeds.

In some places, the path is almost lost from her sight. Many weeds and vines have grown over it. They entangle her feet and legs. No one would bother to keep this path open. As she approaches the burial place, she hears a faint cry. Her heart beats rapidly with renewed hope. For a fleeting moment, she is frozen. She can't make her feet move. Then she moves swiftly through the heavy growth toward the sound. On the ground she sees a large black mass. It's moving re-lentlessly forward. It sweeps over everything in its path. Large black mandibles shine like polished ebony.

"Driver ants!" she exclaims in panic.

They march in a long line. Everything in their path is devoured. She remembers the results of the drivers' visit. Laraba has seen the scant remains of a chicken or duck or the lifeless form of a half-eaten goat. Yet the ant's strong jaws were still pulling away flesh. Fighting off nausea, she follows the line of ants moving toward the crying. In her mind's eye, she can see her babies covered by the driver ants. She gasps for breath. Her heart feels as if it will burst. Her face is flushed and hot. Soon she's going beside the line of ants. Laraba is careful to avoid stepping on them or getting in their path. The load on her head falls to the ground, but she runs on. Her heart races. Tears cloud her eyes. Her legs feel tight. She stumbles, almost falling.

Her fear reaches new heights. She cries out in a panting voice, not caring that she is in the forbidden forest. "Have they already begun to take my babies away from me?"

A Sad Morning

After several hours of restless sleep, Audu awakens, still numb from the happenings of the night and the early morning. He moves from that hut to the one from which he had taken the babies. That's where he had left Laraba. He is apprehensive. Slowly, he enters. His face is furrowed. His hands tremble. The oil in the lamp is out. The windowless room is shrouded in darkness. He squints, trying to penetrate the gloom. As his eyes adjust to the room, he sees Laraba's mat and hoe. Each is in its place. She isn't here. A wave of nausea sweeps over him. Sweat covers his forehead. His body shakes uncontrollably. It feels like it did when he had chills and fever a few months ago. But that was because of the malaria.

"Laraba! Laraba!" he shouts.

He stumbles out into the light. Again, he calls, "Laraba!"

Quickly, he looks around the compound. As he passes between two huts, he almost runs into Uwa. "Where is Laraba?"

"Is she not in her hut?"

"No, she is not there. I cannot find her in the compound."

"Maybe she has gone to the farm."

"No, her hoe is in its place."

"Perhaps she has gone on her own to hide in the bush until this terrible danger is over. That would be quicker and better than waiting for the villagers to drive her out."

"I doubt she would do that, though her impurity is great," blurts out Audu.

"Could she have gone to the river for a bath?" Uwa speaks hesitantly. Then, shaking her head, she adds, "No! I do not think the others would allow her to go there with them."

"I will go there anyway and see," replies Audu.

Reaching the river, he seeks Laraba among the many women bathing and others washing clothes. One woman has her back to Audu. She's pounding her clothes on a rock to remove the dirt. From behind, she looks like Laraba, so he calls to her. Although several look up, no one responds. She isn't at the public bathing place.

He sees his sister, who is talking with some other young girls. He beckons her to come. He quietly asks, "Roda, have you seen Laraba?"

"No, she is not here."

"When did you come?"

"Only a short time ago."

"Have you seen her today?"

"No."

"Are you sure you have not seen her today?"

"Yes, Audu, I am sure."

Others strain to listen. They also question and wonder. They whisper, "Where is Laraba?"

Not finding her at the stream, Audu runs back to his compound. Panting for breath, he calls out to Uwa, "She is not there. Roda and the others have not seen her. Where can she be?"

One of Bako's other wives is busy pounding yam with her pestle in a large mortar. She stops the rhythmic up and down swings to hear what Audu is saying. He squats down beside the cooking area where Uwa is preparing the midday meal.

Suddenly, Audu says to Uwa, "I am going to see if Laraba went to her farm!"

Before Uwa can answer, Audu leaves the compound. As he passes the stalk fence, he brushes against it and almost loses his balance. He doesn't want to meet anyone on his way. So he decides not to go the route that skirts the stream. Instead, he runs along another trail. This makes the trip longer. He goes as fast as he can over the path that is seldom used. It's rough and has interfering growth on both sides. Along the way, he loses his thongs made from old tires, but he keeps running. He hardly realizes he's barefooted. His feet are hard, rough and dry. Audu thinks Laraba probably isn't there. But he must be certain.

Audu reaches Laraba's patch of maize. He senses her presence, even though she isn't there. Everything about the crop reflects her care. Although adjoining other farm plots, hers is noticeably different. The rows are well-contoured to the slope of the land. The fertile topsoil won't wash away. Laraba had removed stones from the nearby fields. She had put them so they would retain the dirt. Other rocks bank a location for a fire and provide sitting places. This completes the border. The pot that holds drinking water is covered. Each plant has received its special attention. This farm is a work of love—Laraba's love.

As he stares at the land outstretched before him, Audu sits down on the ridge Laraba had left at the edge of her farm. His back aches from running. His feet and legs are swollen and hurt from the thorns that caught them along the way. He spreads his legs apart so his elbows can rest on his knees. Raising his arms, he catches his face between his hands. He leans on his fingers with his thumbs on each side of his cheeks. He imagines Laraba's presence. With closed eyes, he sees her with the short-handled hoe in hand. She's bent from her waist to till the dirt. Even with the back-breaking toil, he remembers her smile. It was as if she possessed some knowledge about things that no one else knows.

Audu remembers how much she enjoyed the planting season, the growing time and the harvest. As the plants grew bigger, she shared her contagious enthusiasm with those in their compound. Even though he spent most of his time in the market, he was always touched by her excitement and anticipation of the fruits of her labor. Her enjoyment of life pleased him very much. Gazing out over her small group of plants causes Audu to realize that her corn is almost ready to harvest.

Being here reminds Audu of the first time he and his father brought Laraba to this very place. When they came to a clear spot with a little slope, Bako had said, "This land is good. Crops will be bountiful."

With his foot Bako had put an "X" in the black loam. He placed a small stone on it. Leaning on his stick for support, he had taken slow strides toward the rising sun. After 330 steps, he told Audu to mark the place with a large jagged rock. He turned. This time he took 280 steps. Again, he paused but a moment for Audu to mark that corner. After resting briefly, he turned to measure the next line. Finally, he limped back to the original spot. This designated Laraba's farm plot. It was evident to Audu and Laraba that the most fertile land had been selected. Someone had painstakingly removed the stones and stumps. Although it was beside other small fields, it had been fallow for several seasons. Yet the land was free of any unwanted growth. Even a casual observer would know this was a very special place because someone had given careful attention to its preparation and care.

He remembers Laraba freely expressing her pleasure to Bako and to him. "It is good dirt, and I will tend it faithfully. I must hurry and begin. It will be wonderful to see the new plants burst into life and bloom." Then she danced around and around the two of them as Bako sat resting.

Next, Audu thinks about the excitement he felt as they had their conversations about her crops each growing season. "It is always wonderful to see the tiny plants growing and beginning to bear fruit," she had usually told him.

"Do you expect a good crop this time?" he often asked.

"Yes. The maize I have selected is hearty. I am confident that it will produce in abundance," she always answered.

"Now she is gone," he whispers. He slips from his seat to the ground and begins to rock back and forth. Since there is no one to see him, he allows himself to cry.

"I don't know what to do," he mutters softly. "But I must find Laraba and destroy the twins."

Interrupting his reminiscing are the cries of some grey monkeys jumping from limb to limb in the trees not far away. It jars his thoughts back to the task at hand. He must decide where else to look for Laraba.

It hurts to leave "her place." This intensifies his loneliness and his futile search. He returns to his compound, walking like an old man carrying a heavy load. Audu picks up his sandals along the way. He doesn't speak to those he meets.

CHAPTER SIX

Found At Last

As Laraba runs on the right side of the driver ants' trail, she again hears the sound—it is the cry of babies—behind her and to her left. She whirls around. There they are, lying on the ground—her babies! The ants had passed them by a few feet.

"Ai-e-e-e, Ai-e-e-e," she moans.

Tears run like rivulets through the perspiration on her dust-laden face. She sobs with joy as her heart breaks into intense weeping. She drops heavily to the shadow-covered ground. It has been softened by the light rain. Her knees sink into the earth. Laraba's hands shake as she reaches for her little ones. She clutches her babies to her breast. She can't stop her weeping.

Through her sobs, she whispers, "My little ones, my dear little ones. At last I have found you. Never will I let you go."

How long have I been searching? Oh, so long! But, this hunt cannot be measured in time alone. Her stomach aches with anguish and hunger. *Cannot understand how anyone could think these two tiny ones are evil. It is ridiculous to think that anything so precious could be a threat.*

Swiftly Laraba removes one of the cloths from her waist. She places it on the damp ground. With trembling hands, she tenderly lifts each crying newborn. She cleans their buttocks with some soft leaves and places them on the cloth. Carefully, she bundles them up in her arms, hugging them. Now she returns to where her load of clothes had fallen. After picking them up, she leaves the forbidden bush. It is known for restless spirits.

Finding her babies has renewed her energy. As quickly as she can, she trots along the trail where the sun filters through the cover of leaves. She makes her way from the spot. The babies keep on crying. They are hungry. She seeks a cool place to stop and rest with them.

When she comes to a protected cove, she slips to the ground. Laraba tries to nurse them.

After a short rest, she looks around. There is a water hole a short distance away. She begins to bathe them. Each one screams and shivers in the chilly water. Quickly, she dries them off. They become quiet. She peers carefully into their wee faces. She pushes back a few strains of their tiny black curls as she wraps her arms around both of them and pulls each one to herself. Laying them down, she takes off the cloth she had wrapped around herself and rinses it out. Binding herself with another cloth, she will have to carry the wet one in her hand as she travels. After resting for a while longer, Laraba knows she must decide what to do.

'Cannot return home. Uwa and the other older villagers will never allow me to keep the two. Huh, they will not even let me keep one. She sighed heavily. *Even the younger people follow the customs of our people. Take them to my father's house? No, his village holds the same beliefs. Baba might hide us for a few days. He would not permit two evil ones to remain in his compound very long. He might even force me to destroy them immediately. He would insist they be killed. Not even my father will help me. The only thing for us to do is to go far, far away. Should start right now.*

Again, she sighs, "My sweet little ones, I do not know where we are going. We will not be welcomed at your father's house nor my father's house."

It's hard for her to stand. Only after placing the babies on the ground is she able to struggle to her feet. Gazing down at them, she considers how to carry two little ones. *Easy enough to carry one. Have carried babies for as long as I can remember. Always a little brother or sister or a neighbor's child who needed care in my father's compound. But two? Have never seen that done. No one in my village has ever carried two on her back.*

She picks up one baby, leans forward slightly, and carefully puts it on her back with a leg on each side of her waist and its head lying in the hollow of her back. She wraps a long cloth around its bottom and ties the cloth firmly at her waist. Then she slips it toward the left side and puts the other little one on the right side and ties it on. She puts another cloth around their buttocks covering their backs, legs, and arms. Only their heads peek out above the cloth. As she begins to walk, she's unsteady. That causes her gait to be wobbly. Feeling uncertain, she often reaches under one of the babies. Then she places her hand under the other. She pushes one up to change its position. Immediately she needs to shift the location of the other. She slowly walks on her way. She is concerned that one might fall.

Struggling to walk, Laraba realizes she is very hungry. *Have not eaten today. If I find a farm with ripe harvest, will take some food. Wish I had some way to cook—it would taste better.*

After trudging along for about thirty minutes, she finds some berries she likes. She picks and eats them. Still, she's hungry. In the distance she hears the sound of people talking and drummers drumming. *Not far from a village. Must be market day there. Not my village. Can safely go there to buy some cooked food.* She decides to hide the babies outside the village and slip into town to purchase some food.

"I am so hungry. I need to eat so we can continue our journey," she murmurs softly to her babies.

When she reaches the narrow, two-lane tarmac road, she cautiously looks right and left. No one is there. But she moves farther back into the bush. She finds a shady place beside several large rocks. Gently she lays the sleeping babies together on a cloth. Then she covers them.

As fast as Laraba can walk, she goes to the village. She finds the nearest food seller. The rich smell of soup boiling in a nearby pot makes her realize even more how hungry she is. She can't risk taking time to have a meal. So she bargains for several small freshly fried bean cakes. The palm oil, bubbling in the cook's pot, is waiting for more balls of dough to be dropped in. Receiving her change, she ties it along with her other money in the end of the long cloth that is tucked back under her wrap. Turning to avoid anyone who might pass her way, she trots as fast as she can back to her babies, eating as she goes.

"I must hurry," she admonishes herself. "Something could happen to them while I am away!"

Approaching the hiding place, she hears both of them crying loudly. "Hush, hush, my beautiful ones," she croons as she nears them. Finding they have wet their cloth, Laraba removes it and hangs it on a nearby tree limb to dry, along with her own damp binding cloth. As soon as she nurses them, they fall asleep. Laraba rests. Overcome with fatigue, she spreads some of her cloth on the ground. She quietly lies down on it. Soon she drops off to sleep.

◆　◆　◆　◆　◆

Reaching home after his visit to Laraba's farm, Audu finds Uwa, "Has Laraba returned?" he asks.

"No. No one has seen her."

"Then I must go back to the forbidden bush," he groans. "I must see what has happened there."

Audu retraces his steps along the narrow trail that meanders through the thorn trees and scrub and goes on to the grassland. Then he veers to the right. He hurries along the same route he had traveled the previous night. Finally, trembling and exhausted, he reaches the buttressed roots of the tree in the forbidden forest where he had placed the twins. They are gone! He looks on the far side of the tree. The end of a line of driver ants is marching away from the tree. Scant bones are scattered on the ground nearby. He ponders what had happened. *Did the ants eat the two? Was it the right tree?* It was dark last night, so he thought he might have used another tree. *Was it possible that Laraba found the babies? If so, had she taken them to finish the task?* Perhaps that was it. *How can I be sure?* The rain of the early morning had covered any evidence of what might have happened. Audu can tell nothing. Many other questions fill his mind.

He falls on the ground, breathless. He needs to think. Some would say their disappearance is the work of evil spirits. He feels in his stomach that Laraba has taken the babies. But where had she gone? She knew he was going to destroy the two. She must have known he was doing it for her. A man must do what he knows to be right. He can't expect others to do it for him. He can't wait. If he does, he's always too late. Did Laraba not agree? They had never talked about this. But both knew. Everyone knows what has to be done when twins are born.

He vaguely remembers hearing about his father's third wife who had given birth to two. They were destroyed to avoid disasters. Even so, their mother had died.

After a few minutes, he realizes he might be in danger in this forbidden place. He doesn't want to anger the spirits. Audu leaves. He walks aimlessly away. Breaking the stillness of the bush, he wails, "Laraba, Laraba. Where are you?"

How long he wanders he doesn't know. Still, he finds no trace of Laraba or the babies. He is so mixed up. He doesn't know whether to be sad or relieved. But he knows he is afraid.

His frantic hours of wandering and searching the bush are fruitless. Since he can think of no other places to go this evening, he returns to his compound. Exhausted and dragging his feet, Audu goes in the entrance hut. Uwa meets him.

"Is Laraba here?" he asks.

"No, she has not returned."

Filled with great weariness, he sinks down on a nearby stool. He places his arms across his knees to rest his pounding head. The sun goes down. He hasn't taken food all day. But he can't eat what Uwa has prepared for him.

The news spreads quickly that Audu can't find Laraba. Villagers continue to wonder which disastrous spirit has caused all of this? Many are reluctant to acknowledge the tragedy. Yet all join in the talk. Some even search for Laraba. All question the events of that fateful night.

CHAPTER SEVEN

Broadening His Search

Long before light the next morning, Audu awakens. He slips outside and sinks down, sitting on a log in the yard.

"I have to think. Where would she have gone?" he asks, knowing there would be no answer.

Suddenly, he jumps up and leans against his hut wall. "I will go to see Jato. Perhaps she went to her father's house."

Uwa hears him. She comes to her door. "What did you say?"

"I'm going to Jato's house."

"Will you wait for the sun?"

"No, I must go now."

"But it is still night and time for sleep. It is not safe. The spirits are about. They know about the twins—and you are tired."

Uwa realizes she isn't going to change Audu's mind about leaving before daylight. She prepares some boiled yams and dried meat. He'll have something to eat on the trip to Gundu. She wraps it in paper. Only yesterday that had covered the bright cloth Audu had given to Laraba for the expected child.

With a heavy heart, Audu checks the tires, brakes, and light on his bicycle. Then he rides off into the night. As he approaches the first small village, he punctures the rear tire of his cycle. He pushes it to the repairman's house. He had often been to this village when he first began trading. In his desperation, he is unmindful of the early hour.

"Dogo," he calls impatiently. "Dogo, I need your help!"

"Who is there? What do you want?" bellows Dogo.

"It is I, Audu."

"Where are you going at this time of night? What is the need?"

"To Gundu—I need you to repair my tire." He says no more.

Like a caged animal, Audu paces back and forth. Dogo repairs the tire in the dull light of his small oil lamp. Hurriedly, Audu pays Dogo and resumes his journey. The night is clear, warm, and noisy. Insects lift their voices in chorus. Dogs bark here and there. Audu knows many who live in this little town where he had brought goods like lamps, cycle bells, pots, and pans to sell. Few were interested in buying as they had little money.

Passing near some huts, he hears a child crying and a man coughing. Then, all is silent as he reaches the outskirts of the village. Except for the night creatures, it's quiet and lonely traveling the dark road. His cycle light is dim, so he has to carefully watch the trail ahead. Some of the time he walks, pushing his bicycle because it's too hard to follow the footpath. He feels nervous as he remembers hearing that recently a lion had been seen out this way. He had been told that a hunter killed it with a poisoned arrow. His heart beats faster. He feels the perspiration running down his body under his arms. He wonders what he'll do if he meets a lion or a laughing hyena. Again, he climbs on his bicycle. He peddles as hard and fast as he is able. He strains to see the trail in the darkness. Abruptly, he sees a pile of wood beside the path.

Stopping his cycle, he whispers, "Ah, I will take some of these big, long sticks to help ward off any animal I might meet."

Audu puts down the bicycle's stand. He turns the light toward the stack and looks for a few strong pieces to take. A large twisted piece of metal had been placed across the wood to protect the heap from thieves. "No!" he cries out. "Juju power is here. I can't touch them. Certainly must not take even one!"

Quickly and sadly he returns to his bicycle. He continues his trip down the road again. Several times he stops to listen to the jungle sounds. He feels very tired and begins to wonder if he will be able to finish this journey. It is almost sunrise. Relieved, he finally arrives at his father-in-law's house.

Audu calls to Jato through the darkness. After a few minutes, the door opens just a crack. Looking at Audu with sleepy eyes, Jato pulls the door wide open. He greets his son-in-law.

"Welcome, Audu," Jato says. "How is your house? You have come early. What is the news?"

From his questions, Audu knows Laraba isn't here. A sinking feeling fills his stomach. He sways like a branch blown by the wind as hopelessness saps the last bit of his strength.

"I am looking for Laraba. We have had much trouble," Audu's voice quivers. He neglects to engage in the expected greetings. "Let us sit in your hut. We must not talk where anyone can hear us."

Leading him into the large, cool, round hut, Jato says, "We will sit here."

Exhausted, Audu drops to a mat on the floor.

"Azumi," Jato calls to his wife. "Prepare food. Audu has come." Turning to Audu, he adds, "Now I am ready to hear you."

By Audu's halting words and the frown on his face, Jato knows Audu is carrying much tension and stress. Wringing his hands Audu begins, "Two nights ago Laraba gave birth to twins. I don't know why this evil has come to my house. Quickly, I took them to the forbidden bush. They were placed under a large baobab tree. Its knotted limbs reached out in many strange directions. Returning to my hut, I slept. When I woke up, I went to Laraba's hut. She was not there. I could not find her anywhere in the village. I ran to her farm. She was not there. I returned to the forbidden forest and looked under the tree where I left the twins. They were gone. I have looked everywhere for them. I have not been able to find them. I came here hoping Laraba had come here and was with you."

In a strained voice, Jato speaks, "Why? For what cause has this come?" His voice breaks, "Why? Why?" He had longed for his daughter to give her husband a son and many other children. How had this happened?

After a period of silence, he blurts out, "The evil ones must be angered!"

"Yes, but why?"

After more conversation, Azumi enters with food. Pausing, she looks from Audu to Jato. Without speaking, she places the colorful red, black and white enamel bowl of hot food on the mat in front of them and leaves the room.

"What are we to do? Where, oh, where is Laraba? And have the babies been destroyed?" Audu moans.

"I too do not know," answers Jato, shaking his head. He leans over and places his hand on Audu's shoulder, "She will return. I know she will return. Perhaps she went to finish the task."

"If so, would she not have come back by now?"

"But, where could she have gone?"

"I wish I knew!"

"Let me think," Jato begs. After sitting quietly with his head in his hand he finally questions, "Did she take any cloth? Did she have money?"

"No, no," Audu replies. "I don't think she took much with her. Her hut was in order."

"Did you look in her box?"

"No, but there could not have been much money. None of the crop has been sold this season. I do not know how much money she may have saved."

"Perhaps she will return after she has finished her task," Jato suggests again.

"I do not believe she will take the lives of the little ones," declares Audu. "She loves life too much to do that. She will want to keep them."

"Yes, I know. But she knows they are different and must be destroyed. She knows the trouble they bring with them. Will she not be afraid to keep them?" her father argues.

"Yes, I am sure she is afraid. Besides where can she go with them?"

"And who will help her if she keeps the babies? All of our people fear them."

"I do not know! How I wish I knew! If only the gods were not so cruel!"

"Speak with care!" Jato cautions. After a long interval of strained silence Jato speaks again. "We must make inquiries in the surrounding villages to see what we can learn. Laraba may have gone to one of them. She might feel safe where she is not known. She cannot bring them here or back to your house. All know that two bring tragedy."

"If any news comes, you will send word to me?" pleads Audu. When Jato nods his head in agreement, Audu responds, "Thank you, thank you."

"Surely she has done the job and will return soon. Of all my children, Laraba has always taken her responsibilities most seriously. Do those of your village know she is gone?"

"Yes, some of them joined me in the search."

"Ah, Audu, why has this threatening thing come? Never do I remember this happening in my father's house or his father's."

"I do not know."

"We will not tell anyone here of the evil that has come to you," Jato warns.

"Whatever you say. It is midday and I must go."

The food is left untouched, as Audu stands to leave and return home.

"Go well, Audu," Jato speaks with longing.

Audu again mounts his bicycle and begins his journey home. Many he knows speak to him as he leaves, but he hardly sees them or cares. Some turn to look after him, wondering about his unusual behavior.

The return trip is long and tedious. The anguish he feels and his lack of food and sleep make him weary. Going up some of the small hills becomes increasingly difficult. Several times he has to stop riding. Then, he walks with the cycle. The calves of his legs grow tight. He gets off his bicycle to rub them to ease the discomfort. Standing in the middle of the trail, he rests his head on the handlebars. He must go on. But he hardly has enough energy to pedal. Halfway home, Audu remembers the food that Uwa had sent with him. He sits for a while under the shade of a tall, thick, green-leaved mango tree. The food is tasteless, but he forces himself to eat. After eating and resting, he feels better and continues his trip home.

As he travels he can think of nothing but Laraba and the twins. He questions everything that has happened. He even remembers how soft and tiny the babies were. He thought he had put their bodies completely out of his mind. *Were they boys, or a boy and a girl, or simply two girls?* He wishes he'd at least discovered that before he left them in the forbidden forest. Knowing he shouldn't even think about them, he forces himself to think of something else. Immediately, Laraba comes to mind. He had never before considered how great his affections for her had become. When she came as his wife, she only satisfied him. He didn't even know her. She was just his wife who was to be the mother of his children. But as time passed, he realized that he began to care for her deeply. Now that she's gone, he realizes he misses her very much. Thinking about her and the possibility that she might have returned home makes the remainder of his trip bearable. As night approaches, Audu finally reaches his compound. Uwa meets him.

"Did you find her?" she anxiously questions.

Audu shakes his head sadly. From his mother's question, he knows Laraba hasn't returned home. He feels an urge to cry. But he stifles the tears. He's been searching for Laraba and the twins to be sure the infants were destroyed. Now he realizes he wants to find Laraba because he loves her. He keeps wondering where she has gone. Why did she go? Had the strenuous effort of birth weakened her mind? Maybe she isn't responsible. That only adds to his anxiety. He had never felt so helpless. He felt enclosed in a cage of depression because of the dreads of life.

CHAPTER EIGHT

Unplanned Journey

When Laraba awakens from her nap under a tree beside her twins, night has arrived. The moon gives a little light. It is too dark for Laraba to see well enough to walk any farther. There is no place to go to be safe. So she spreads the remainder of her cloth she'd been carrying on the gritty, rough ground. Lying down with her arm across her babies, she wonders about tomorrow. She shivers. Will they survive the night? Where will she go in the morning? Even being very uneasy, her weariness won't allow her to stay awake. Her sleep is restless, disturbed by the strange sounds of hyenas and bush dogs calling to each other in the night.

From time to time, the babies cry. She wakes up and cares for them. Once during the night, she awakens with perspiration soaking her body because of a terrifying nightmare. She sees her babies floating down the river out of her reach. In the moonlight, she looks around in dismay.

"Where am I? Why am I in this place?" she moans, as confusion fogs her thinking.

Then with a smile, Laraba remembers where she is. Her adorable babies are close beside her. They're crying but are no longer lost. They are alive and safe with their mother. Again, she cleans them up and sits on the ground to nurse them. One continues to cry, so Laraba cradles it in her arms. She rocks back and forth until sleep comes. When both are quiet, she knows that as soon as light appears, she must decide where to go. Lying back on the hard ground, she soon dozes off again.

Shortly before daylight, a morning dove awakens her with its song. As soon as she can see more clearly, she sits up and struggles to get to her feet. Her arms and legs are sore and stiff. After several attempts, she is able to stand. She takes two cloths to tie the babies in their places against her body. As she tries to put both infants where they had been before, she thinks, *Awkward! Uncomfortable for me and them. What would be better? One on my back. One in front.*

Laraba places one in front and ties a cloth around the baby's buttocks and herself. Then, she picks up the second by one of its arms, leans slightly forward, and slings it onto her back. She ties another cloth around it and herself. Except for their heads, the babies' entire bodies are covered. Feeling them snuggled up close to her, each in its own spot and comfortable, she smiles. *Better. This is the way.*

She removes the now dried cloths from the tree limb, where she had hung them last night. Laraba puts one over her shoulder. The other one is placed with her bundle of clothes that she carries on her head. She goes up near the road and starts walking in the bush a few feet from it.

For a while, she walks on. She has to stop occasionally to rest and nurse the babies. Her journey becomes tedious. Her feet are dragging. Her head aches. Laraba stops. She is too tired to go on. A longer rest is needed. She puts some cloth on the ground in the shade of an umbrella tree. Her weary arms and hands remove the babies from their places. As she lays each one down, she gently hugs it. While the two sleep, she examines them closely. She carefully strokes their faces. Her loving eyes fill with tears of joy.

Her hand trembles as she moves it over their bodies. Not quite touching them but, oh, so close. "Their tiny hands and feet are perfectly formed," she boasts softly. *What is wrong with two?* She is extremely perplexed. As she looks at them now, she doesn't know which had been born first. One is not more or less her baby than the other. Why then are two unwanted? Why had the birth of the second caused the first to be undesirable and both to be evil? Since their birth, she hasn't been able to sort out her feelings. Nor can she understand the logic of her peoples' customs about twins. She is torn between the beliefs of her people and the feelings in her heart. Many unanswered questions remain.

Suddenly she again thinks. *They are not evil but wonderful!* Her heart sings. Never had she seen anything as exciting and beautiful. Her concerns hold no meaning for her now. She looks up as two finches flutter away and a red bishop lands on a limb near her head.

She speaks aloud without realizing it, "I know Audu would agree with me that they are not evil, if only he could look at them one moment without fear."

But Laraba can't afford to confront Audu with this possibility. She must tend to the present needs of these two wonderful little ones. *Where to go with two babies?* She ponders their precarious plight. Unexpectedly, she remembers her visit to the city of Danbar. Several years had passed since Laraba went there with her father, Jato. They'd gone to a house on Pump Street intending to visit kinfolks, but the family had moved. In their place, they found John and Victoria, who were from a neighboring village. She had never forgotten them. They were kind. Victoria was expecting a baby. John helped her father locate someone in their family. *They welcomed us without reservations. They treated us like their own family. Have never met anyone like them before or since. Only with them a couple of days. Enough time to be certain that in this difficult situation, they will help me.*

"Yes," she whispers, "John and Victoria will help us. We must go to Danbar."

With renewed determination, Laraba stands. She ties the babies on her body. Then she places her bundle of clothes on her head and moves from the bush to the road. A cloud of dust announces the approach of a dull brown lorry with the inscription "No telephone to Heaven" written across the top of the cab. It slowly comes to the top of the hill. Although she is gripped with fear, she waves frantically. Then she takes the large body cloth that was across her shoulders and wraps it around her neck so that it flows sweepingly down over the twins. Fortunately, the driver sees her and stops.

Leaning from the window, he smiles and speaks to her. "What may I do for you?'

"Where is this lorry going?"

"To Danbar. Would you like a ride?"

"Yes, what is the cost?"

"Ordinarily, it would be three shillings, three pence, but for you I will charge only three shillings, two pence."

"That is very dear, but I must travel to Danbar." Without further discussion, she selects a few coins.

After she pays what the driver demanded (more than the fare should be), she goes to the back of the mammy wagon. She struggles up the three steps to climb aboard. Laraba weaves her way around some bags belonging to other passengers. They are sprawled out, trying to sleep. She steps over their feet and legs and takes the only place she sees to sit.

Laraba again adjusts the cloth on her shoulders to hide the babies. She doesn't want to be stopped now. No one pays any attention to her as she boards. Most of them have traveled many long, hard hours. The warm air, heavy dust, and dirt have drained them of their alertness. Many were asleep until they stopped. The jolt awakens them for only a few seconds until they determine they must still travel farther. Then, they again lean up against the side of the lorry or the bags of goods and go back to sleep. All suffer from bodily and mental exertion.

Slowly, the old Mercedes picks up speed. Laraba shifts on her hard plank on the side of the lorry, trying to get comfortable. She has to lean forward to protect the baby on her back. Her body is sore, but she dares not complain. Carefully, she rearranges her twins into a more restful position. She is glad they are asleep. No one seems to notice them. Soon enough, she expects to face the hostility from some of the other passengers who might join them for a ride to town. Now she must relax if she and her babies are to safely complete this long trip. Even though the road is rough and dusty and the lorry swerves from time to time, she soon sleeps. Several times the driver stops along the way to allow others to board, until there is no more room.

At one of the stops, the babies start crying. Laraba quickly works to allow them to nurse and tries to comfort them. She has trouble getting them to be quiet. A thin, old woman sitting across from her slips from her seat and moves to the small place beside Laraba. She pushes her way in between Laraba and the traveler sitting beside her. Watching the woman, Laraba is puzzled by her actions and curious about what she might do.

The woman greets Laraba, warmly asking, "Are they twins? How old are your babies?"

Concerned about the reaction of the people on the lorry, Laraba hesitantly and quietly replies, "Yes. Just a few days old."

"Where are you going with such new babies?"

Laraba answers in a hushed voice, "To Danbar to see some friends."

"May I help you care for them as we travel? I will leave the lorry a short while before the city, but I can hold one until then. This will help you sit more comfortably on these rough boards."

"Thank you," Laraba whispers, doubting if she is wise to accept this help.

Trying to relieve the terror the woman sees in Laraba's eyes, she smiles broadly. Then she adds, "I am a grandmother. I have cared for many babies. You have two beautiful babies. I would enjoy helping you with them while we travel."

Those sitting nearby strain to hear their conversation. Word is passed down to the other passengers. This promotes many of the people to begin talking about children, especially babies. Some want to see the twins. A chill shakes Laraba's body whenever anyone looks at them. Several are speaking to each other in various languages she doesn't know, and Laraba fears what they are saying. *Is anyone from my people group on this lorry, or someone who might know my customs?*

Finally, a man silences the others by speaking loudly in the trade language of the area, which the others understand. He wants to tell them about his recent visit home. Some people near his village have the custom of killing a baby whose upper teeth come in before the lower ones. They believe that great evil will come upon its family if the child isn't killed.

"Who kills the baby? How is it done?" inquires another person.

"The mother is responsible."

"I've heard that too," interrupts the woman sitting beside Laraba, who is holding one of the twins. Laraba stiffens, wondering what else she knows.

"How does she kill such a baby?" asks the man with mud-red tattoos decorating his palms and the soles of his feet, who is sitting across from Laraba.

"There are usually two possibilities. One is to give it a drink and then strangle it. The other is to wrap it tightly at night so it smothers."

Shaking their heads, several speak gravely, "Ayee, ayee." Laraba quivers.

After the excitement of the last few miles and the heated discussion about babies, the trip becomes dull again. The lorry travels along undisturbed. Everyone seems to be deep in thought. Laraba is grateful for the quietness and especially that the babies are silent. But she remains uncertain what might happen before this trip is concluded.

Another time, when they pick up some more riders, someone in the back calls to the driver, "There is no more room!"

But the driver pays no attention and says to the two men, "Climb in the back and find a place to sit. There is room."

Finally, the lorry driver stops to allow himself and the passengers to ease themselves on the side of the road. Laraba always stays to herself and only responds if someone speaks directly to her. When they come to a market place, the driver pulls over to purchase gasoline.

The owner quickly states, "Petrol no da."

A passenger calls to the driver, "Make you give chance to get chop."

But the driver tells him, "No, wait until the next place. You can get food while I get petrol. Several passengers plan to leave us there." He starts the engine and drives off.

At the next town, the driver pulls over to get gas. Those who are hungry want to purchase something to eat. They walk across the road. Stalls with food for sale are over there. The passengers buy food and quickly return. Still eating, they climb back into the lorry. Laraba purchases several pieces of fried plantain. She returns to the lorry, finds her seat, and begins eating.

Her new friend gently hands Laraba the twin she has been holding and says, "I leave you here. Take care of these precious babies. I hope you arrive safely and find your friends well."

As the old woman shoves her loads from the lorry, Laraba breathes a sigh of relief. She smiles and tells her, "Thank you for your help. Go well."

A man, a woman, two children, three chickens with their feet tied together, and a goat held by a short, well-worn rope, replace the ones who left the lorry. After more rough riding, the long arduous trip is ended, as they reach Danbar. The truck enters Lorry Park Number Three. It comes to a stop beside other vehicles waiting to be loaded or unloaded. Stiff and tired, Laraba climbs down from the lorry. Vividly recalling her visit several years ago, she remembers the address clearly—24/5 Pump Street. But she doesn't remember the direction from the lorry park.

Although she is hesitant to speak to him, she asks the driver, "Can you direct me to Pump Street?"

With arrogance, he glares at her and responds, "No, I am not from this place and seldom visit it, except to drive my lorry here." Then he warmly adds, "But I know a place you can stay for the night. Just come with me."

"No, I must find Pump Street. Someone I know lives there."

"Then why are they not here to meet you, so you can follow them home?"

Becoming agitated and concerned, Laraba quickly turns away, as she replies, "Perhaps they will come soon."

Others hurry away before she can inquire of them. Her legs resist normal movement, but slowly respond as she forces one foot and then the other to move. Seeing a hand pump, she stops for a drink of water. Then she goes in the direction she sees many of the people walking. Entering the main part of the city, she looks around. Things are strange. *So different from my village.* She searches hesitantly through the lonely and deserted streets.

Where now? This place is not like I remember. Have they moved the lorry park? This light is fast fading. Turning right, she sees the night market that is still open. Laraba walks through the darkness to where many lights flicker around the area. Some are little kerosene-burning lamps made from small tin cans. Once they had held Peak brand sweetened condensed milk, imported from Holland. Their wicks are stuck through a hole in the center of the top of the can. Even so, they struggle to absorb enough fuel to burn. Others are miniature clay bowls filled with palm oil, containing wicks made from twisted cloth. They all sit upon boxes or tables containing goods for sale. *This must be the big market in Danbar. Maybe a trader will help me.*

Stopping at the first stall, Laraba says, "Good evening. How are you?"

The women, from behind a few piles of tomatoes and onions, replies, "Good evening. I am fine. How are you?"

"I am well. Is business good?"

"Yes, business is very good. What would you like to buy tonight?"

"I cannot purchase anything yet. But perhaps you can direct me to Pump Street."

"No, I do not know that place."

"Thank you," Laraba says in a trembling voice.

She goes further into the market. *Purchase something. Someone will help. Growing late. Must find John and Victoria's house. A banana would taste good. Where is a banana woman?* At that moment one of the babies stirs.

"I should get away from here," she whispers to herself as the other baby begins to wiggle. She quickly goes back the way she came. "I will find a place for you to relieve yourselves. You must be hungry too," she adds, as she pats them on their backs.

After a brief stop, Laraba returns to the market. She seeks a fruit seller, planning to purchase a banana. She hopes the trader will help her find her way. Although the trader doesn't want to sell only one banana, she finally agrees. They dicker over and settle on a price.

Then Laraba casually asks, "Do you know the location of Pump Street?"

"Yes, it is many poles from here." Pointing with her chin, she says, "Go back out of the market, turn toward Barclay's Bank, walk four streets and turn toward the biggest street in town. From there it is only a few blocks away. You will see the road."

How do I follow her directions? Don't want to show my ignorance. She should not know I am a stranger here. Act like I understand her. Maybe the street will appear. So she says, "Thank you, thank you," as she walks out of the market, eating her banana.

When she reaches the road, she turns right like the woman had told her. *What is a bank? Where is it? What are poles?* She decides to look for the big street. After making several turns, Laraba doesn't see it. She tries to retrace her route, looking carefully as she crosses each road.

"Babies, I am very tired," she quietly states, as she stumbles along. "But I am grateful you are asleep now."

After wandering around for some time without seeing anyone, she finally goes up to a building. She leans her left shoulder against it to rest. "Will I ever find Pump Street?" she pleads to the babies.

Suddenly, she sees a street sign straight ahead and discovers she is on Pump Street. Slowly, she starts down the road, trying to see the numbers. They are all faded and dirty. Laraba has to get close to each house. She carefully examines the numbers to determine what they are. She doesn't remember exactly how John and Victoria's house looks. In the dim light, every house seems just like all the others. After she has searched seven houses on each side of the lane, at last, weary relief comes.

"Ahhh," she sighs. "Here it is: number 24/5. This is the house."

The building is dark. Lifting her heavy hand with a tired arm, she knocks several times on the door. Her heart is pounding. *What if they are not here? What will I do? Where will I go?*

"Who is it? Who is there?" a pleasant, but anxious voice calls through the closed door.

"Victoria, it is I, Laraba," she answers with a dry mouth and trembling lips.

Light filters around the door. Then it opens, as Victoria exclaims, "Laraba! Come in. How are you? How is your father? Is he with you?"

"No, my father is at home. I come for your help—I did not know where else to go." Laraba speaks in a hesitant, yet urgent voice. She's unsure how to tell Victoria about her problem.

"Why are you so frightened? Are there many thieves on the streets? Has someone bothered you?"

"No. This—is—the—reason," she responds, as she removes the flowing garment which hides the twins.

Victoria's dark eyes open wide as she sees the two sleeping babies, "OH! NO!" she gasps, "It cannot be!"

A chill travels down Laraba's spine. Tears fill her eyes. *Have I come to the wrong place? Will they turn me away? Will they send us back to Audu? To his family? To that village? Worse, will they take the babies? Will they drown them?*

CHAPTER NINE

The Lonely Hunt Continues

From time to time, Audu hears the cruel, gossiping whispers of the old women as they discuss the cause of the evil they expect. "Audu's weakness is the reason. He failed to demonstrate his faithfulness to the ways of our people."

"Laraba, even as a young bride, was not kept in check. Never was Audu heard to command her to go quickly to her work or to bring food," adds a toothless old woman.

Another speaks up, "Yes, he neglected to control her. Is this trouble not to be expected from such disregard?"

"They have never shown respect for the things of our people. It is their loss, but we will all suffer because of what they have done."

As they drone on and on, Audu shows restraint. He suppresses his anger. He knows responding to them will serve no purpose. To say nothing is best.

◆ ◆ ◆ ◆ ◆

Early one evening, Audu and Uwa sit together in their compound only speaking when each feels the need to do so. The night is bright with many stars. It's still but not quiet, because the drummers are busy. A short distance away, some of the villagers are woefully singing and talking. In the days before this, those in Audu's compound often joined the group. Now they aren't welcomed. In the distance, other drums are heard. A star shoots across the sky. Soon it is gone.

Where did it go? As he sits with his chin cupped in his hand and stares out into the night, Audu asks, "Did you see the falling one?"

"No, I did not see it," his mother replies.

"I saw it, now it is gone. Just like Laraba—gone. What is life now? It has no meaning without her. How I wish she had spoken to me. I only did what had to be done. Did she not know to trust me?" His torment is reflected in his hoarse voice. Every muscle and nerve in his body aches, drawn as tight as the drum heads echoing around him.

With deep concern, Uwa's quivering voice pleads with Audu, "You must eat and rest. She will return."

Avoiding an answer, he begs, "Help me. I heard about Baba's number three wife and her death. But I was too young to remember it all."

"It is true that she died in childbirth after having twins. They were soon destroyed. There was much trouble afterwards. The crops were not good. We had trouble having enough food. Tools, cloth and other things disappeared in the market. Even with the juju priest's protection put on goods, something happened to many of them. But your father was too busy caring for all the family. He would never talk about it."

"But why? Why?" Audu continues to question.

"It is as it always has been. Twins bring much pain and unhappiness for the family and the village."

After pondering this information for several minutes, Audu struggles to get up. He walks slowly to his hut with his head down. Uwa is left sitting alone.

Her thoughts wing to a day long ago when she'd been in the market. She'd been sitting beside the goods she was selling. It was a bright, hot, dry day. Few were there. Audu was a small boy sleeping on a mat. Flies bothered him. His naked body moved restlessly. Uwa had fanned him with a cow-tail switch.

A stooped, gray-haired man had come up. He bought a small can of milk. He was friendly and soft-spoken, unlike many of the men in the market. He looked lovingly at Audu. Pointing to the leather amulets around his waist, the man had asked, "Why do you place these things about him? They are of no use to you or your son. I can tell you of one who will bless his life and yours. Something that is good forever."

The man spoke foolishly. Uwa just looked away. He continued to stand and gaze at Audu. Finally, she said, "Well, tell me what you speak of. Tell me how to be blessed forever."

The ancient one said, "I will be happy to tell you. I will tell you about a man. He is the Son of God." He told an unusual story, which she didn't believe. It was strange. He didn't believe in amulets. The man didn't criticize her for placing the medicine about Audu's waist. He only said, 'I know a better way. If you trust Him, you will not need the amulets.'"

Uwa can't remember the name of the one he had told her she should trust. She questions if she should have listened more carefully. The old man was of a spirit she didn't know. His interest and concern seemed genuine. He was kind.

She wished she had heeded. There might be a stronger medicine. Would it have made a difference? Staring at the ground, Uwa continues thinking. Why did I not inquire further? It is too late.

◆　◆　◆　◆　◆

Audu decides to visit nearby Quarry Town, hoping to learn something helpful. Perhaps Laraba went there, as it's not far away. Or maybe someone in the village has seen her.

In that place the houses are built close together. There are no yards in which the children can play. With no trees for shade, the dusty road provides the only place for them to kick their balls. Another favorite game for the boys is to roll well-worn bicycle rims along a path, guiding each with a slender stick. It's hard to keep it in the narrow ridges so they can run with speed and safety along the rough surface.

Audu arrives after the men and women return from work. It's time for the evening meal of soup and rice. One of the villagers invites him to eat with them. As he sits in that compound, he sees flames.

A man runs up screaming, "Fire, fire!"

"It is getting closer!" One cries with pain and frustration.

"Get your buckets! Hurry! Hurry!"

Everyone jumps up, grabs the nearest container and races to the well or the one faucet. The cover on the well is securely locked. No one can find the key nor does anyone suggest breaking the lock. The water, as always, comes only in a trickle from the faucet, which the expatriates had put in the village many years ago when tin mining was regularly pursued. The curses heaped upon it do nothing to increase the flow. As their buckets are slowly filled, men, women, boys and girls run to already burning huts. They do no good. It's too little and too late. They are helpless in this crisis.

Glowing sparks dance in the darkness about the village. The fire leaps from hut to hut. Its route is unpredictable. Audu watches thatched roofs and tin ones fall into the huts. The fire consumes all in its path. Before the flames even finish devouring one block of houses, they move to others. Sleeping mats, bed covers, clothes, a few dishes, tables, chairs, and the little personal items collected through the years, such as necklaces, a new broad-toothed comb, a family photo, the water pot and its cover, are gone, quickly destroyed.

The reflection of the fire shines upon the furrowed faces of those who stand silently watching. The crowd follows the path of the fire. Soon the destruction is almost complete.

The villagers now ignore the challenge of the fire. Gone are their possessions. Even greater is their loss of hope and purpose. Audu feels their desperation as he watches them. He sees it mirrored in their large, empty eyes. They stare off into space. Little is said. There is nothing to say. Three sit huddled together, a man and two women. The man is quiet. Tears roll from the women's eyes. A box, a bucket and a few pieces of clothing are all they had been able to save. Others poke around in the still smoldering ruins. Not much that is useful can be recovered. Yet they search.

Flames brighten the sky. Those who look up see low, heavy clouds. They hang above them filled with rain. Then a bitter irony— raindrops begin to fall. Those left impoverished and suffering from the fire are now drenched by the falling rain. The devastation is complete. *Where can they go? What will happen to them? What hope do they have?*

Leaving the burned area, Audu carries the disaster of the fire in his mind and heart. It joins his personal tragedy. Grief from the night the two were born. This one, the calamity of the fire, he'll not carry for long. It doesn't belong to him as the other does. But for now, he struggles with it. Faces hang before him. Those bewildered expressions glowing from the light of doom. No one had asked how the fire started. That made no difference afterwards.

Audu's feet are heavy. His back aches. He is trapped by a sense of the futility of life. You sweat and toil, but to what avail? People can touch so little around them while on this earth. Danger is every- where. There isn't much he can do to help himself or anyone else. In despair, he slowly splashes through the puddles of water, as he walks back down the long, lonely road in the rain. His eyes see only the road. He's overcome with the feeling that his visit to Quarry Town has ended in violence. Fire, the helper of humans, had risen up and quickly run wild. It consumes everything in its path. Glancing back, he sees nothing but a black sky over the village. The fire is gone.

While the tragedy of the fire greatly hurt the villagers, his visit there has done nothing to relieve his concerns. He didn't learn anything about Laraba or the two. His longing for her is intense. He wonders if she is close enough to see the glow of the flames.

◆ ◆ ◆ ◆ ◆

Audu goes to the villages in all directions. He even visits the small ones where only a few families live and farm. In some of those places, he sees many who are suffering from the energy-sapping Guinea worm disease. People sit or lie around, unable to do anything. The whitish worms are in various stages of the slow process of emerging from the terrible, painful, feverish blisters on the feet or legs of their victims. Removal of the two to three-foot-long, thin worm begins when its head appears. It's gradually and carefully wrapped around a strong stick each day until it is too painful for the person to tolerate. This continues until it has completely exited the person's body. It takes weeks to eliminate these worms. He notices one small boy who has several worms emerging from his legs. He is repulsed by the prevalence of the Guinea worm in these villages. But his major concern always returns to his desperate need to find Laraba. He can't imagine that she'd stay in one of those villages, so he doesn't remain long in any of them.

Audu spends his days almost sick with loneliness and longing. He often sits in the edge of the market near the motor park. There he can watch people coming and going. He questions many travelers.

"Have you seen a woman with twins?" He asks the owner of a lorry that pulls into the space near him.

"No, I have not."

Turning to the passengers, he questions, "Have you seen a women with two babies?"

One man says, "Yes, I have seen several women with twins in my city, but not here."

Another person, who came to visit family members, scoffs at Audu and angrily responds, "Why do you ask such a foolish question. You know twins are dangerous!"

Some people, who are only looking for transportation to distant towns, turn away. They have heard of his trouble but won't answer him. A few strangers carry loads of goods on their heads to sell in the market. They shake their heads and move on. Neither the drivers nor the passengers will admit seeing her. He continues to ponder what to do and where to go. He believes the evil from the twins clouds his mind. He can't think.

Often Audu questions the police. They either have no word, or they will not tell him anything. Again he travels to Gundu. Still Jato knows nothing. She hasn't contacted him. Fellow villagers avoid him whenever he leaves his compound. His mental pain becomes more intense. He thinks of nothing but his loss. He tries to stand and walk straight and tall, hoping his suffering will be less visible.

As he is returning home from one of the villages, the rain soaks his body. He hardly notices. He's consumed with his thoughts of Laraba. Audu thinks about Laraba with her hoe in hand on the way to the farm. He imagines her expertly balancing the water pot on her head as she returns from the stream. It's pleasant to imagine her sitting on a three-legged stool outside Uwa's hut. He hears her laughter. He feels her long, slender fingers working their way up his neck. Then she tenderly holds his head in her soothing hands. She whispers, "I am glad to be your wife. You are a good husband."

But when he comes to his compound, she isn't here. He slumps on a stool just outside the door of his hut.

"How did your day go?" his mother asks.

"As usual," he grunts.

"Where will you look now?"

"Where does one go?"

"You need to eat. Let me get you some soup."

"Not hungry," Audu retorts.

Much of the time, he hardly speaks to his mother, even when she asks him a question. He ignores others in his compound. With his head down, he slowly moves from his hut—to the market—to his hut. He wants to avoid the villagers' scornful remarks. So he moves the goods he has for sale. His stall is placed on the other side of the market. Audu travels another way to his booth. Those who know him in the market shun him. He is seldom at his business, so he has little success with his sales. The days slowly pass. But no word comes. Sleep brings little rest. He eats almost nothing. There is no joy in living.

Audu begins to feel that Laraba will not likely return. He realizes that it may be impossible to find her. But maybe she'll decide to let him know where she is. As he walks the long, lonely, dirt roads, he often wonders if Laraba might have boarded a lorry here. She must be far away. Three can't hide. They need friends. They need food. With whom can they stay? Are they still alive? He considers other places where they might be.

Monotonously, day follows day until several weeks pass since Laraba disappeared. Then a plan begins to take shape in Audu's mind.

CHAPTER TEN

Safe at Last

"Sit there." Victoria tells Laraba.

Her red eyes filled with sadness, a haggard Laraba sinks into the chair indicated by Victoria. The front room is dimly lit with one naked bulb dangling from the ceiling. The babies begin to cry. Laraba places one of them to her sore breast. Fatigue helps dull the pain, but tears overrun her eyes. *Have I made a mistake coming here? What will we do then?*

Recovering from her shock and leaving the room, Victoria remarks, "I will bring you food and water."

"Thank you, thank you."

As Laraba cares for the children, she begins to feel more at ease. *Victoria did not scold me! She did not question my decision. Perhaps we will be safe here.* When the infants finally sleep, Laraba eats and drinks. Then she recounts for Victoria all that had happened.

"I am here because I did not know where else to go," she repeats. "It all happened so quickly. After finding the babies where Audu had left them I could not go home. Nor to my father's."

"Yes, I know," agrees Victoria, as she frowns and nods.

Laraba speaks with even more urgency, "I remember how kind you and John were to my father and me when we visited you some years ago. Will you help me and my babies?"

"Oh, yes! You are welcome in our home. I am happy you are here. I am sure John will be glad you came to us, too. You must be very weak and tired after the birth, your long search and rough ride here—such a terrible time." She shakes her head in disbelief. "You need to sleep. You and your babies are safe here. John and I have wanted a child in our home for such a long time. Now there are two. It is good!"

"What about the baby you were expecting when my father and I were here?" Laraba hesitantly asks.

"It died." Victoria spoke so sadly that Laraba could hardly hear her.

"I am sorry."

"Now you must rest," Victoria says softly. "Do not worry. I will care for the babies."

Although fatigue overcomes her body, the ache in her heart eases for the first time since the two were born. The struggle of the last two days begins to fade as she feels safe enough to relax. Released from much of her anxiety, Laraba is soon asleep on a mat placed on the floor in the front room. She sleeps so soundly that even when the babies awaken and cry, she doesn't hear them.

Victoria tenderly cares for them. While they sleep, she goes to a box in her room. With shaking hands, she turns the key that opens the small lock. She lifts the top and removes the paper covering a few small gowns, dresses, blankets, and cloth. Tenderly, she places the valued goods on a clean mat. There are also bottles, nipples, and a brush for cleaning them. She remembers the old women had chided her when she bought these things from the Lebanese shop.

"What need will you have of such things?" they had asked.

Returning part of the clothes to their place, she keeps out some things. As she locks the box, she decides to use these for Laraba's babies. She washes the bottles and nipples. She was overjoyed when she bought those things. That didn't last long. Three times she gave birth. One lived only a few days. Two died at birth. Now she is happy to have babies in her home. She thanks God for the goodness of having these precious little ones. She begins to hum.

Laraba's sleep is restless. Her legs jerk occasionally, as if she is running. But she doesn't wake up. Soon after daylight, John, Victoria's husband, returns home. Victoria can hardly wait to tell him about all that had happened during the night. As John removes his coat and sits to eat, she gives him some porridge and begins, "Do you remember Jato and his daughter, Laraba? They visited us some years ago."

"Yes, I remember them well."

"Laraba is here with twins. Her husband took them to the forbidden forest. He could not finish the task. She recovered them, but did not know where to go until she thought of us. She is resting in the front room. I took care of the babies throughout the night. I bathed them and clothed them in the clean new gowns I had in my box."

As John eats, he listens intently, clicking his tongue with each new bit of information.

"Whenever the babies cried in the night, I quickly cared for them before they could disturb Laraba. I mixed some powdered milk with water in my small calabash. They would not suck from the bottle. So putting my finger into the container I got a few drops of milk. Then I put my finger into their mouths. I was able to get them to take a little nourishment. It was enough to satisfy them for a little while. Once I tied one of them on my back and swayed from side to side until it drifted off to sleep. The babies are so sweet, tender, and beautiful. I told Laraba that she and the babies could stay here." Almost breathless from her stream of conversation, she looks at John for approval.

◆　◆　◆　◆　◆

"Laraba is welcome to stay here with us," John agrees with Victoria. "It will be difficult. But we will care for her and the twins."

John is a tall, big man with broad shoulders. He doesn't wear tribal marks, so his brown face is smooth. He enjoys learning. His eyes are bright when he talks about new things. He is strong, kind, and reliable. The night job of guarding the property of a family while they sleep brings him pleasure. His broad smile is contagious. He's well known for his cheerful words. The children in their neighborhood call out to him when he walks by. Most people he knows greet him quickly, and they enjoy stopping for an exhilarating conversation with him.

Many of the other watchmen get some sleep during their night jobs, because they work another job during the day. But John's normal routine is to return home in the early morning. He eats, then sleeps, and after several hours of rest, he studies. His schooling was cut short by the death of his father. Since he's the oldest son, the responsibility of caring for his mother and the younger siblings has fallen upon him. Now he's helping two of his brothers go to school. Both of them live with John and Victoria in their small house. Fees, uniforms, food and books are expensive, but the satisfaction from helping them is well worth all the effort and sacrifice.

The loss of his own children and the news from the doctor that Victoria will never have a child causes him great anguish. Trying to console him, his friends say, "Take another wife, one who can bear you children. It is good for a man to have many children. If Victoria cannot have any, take a wife who can."

He won't do as they advise. Early in life he had been confronted with this decision. He took his stand against polygamy, as his father had done before him. Many of the young men of his village plan for more than one wife. It's the custom, like many of their fathers before them. Though they are poor, they will manage to have several wives.

Twins! Twins! John looks over at the two sleeping peacefully on their cloth. Walking quietly over to them, he kneels down. He touches the infants. They are very tiny. Their tenderness thrills him as he gently caresses first one and then the other. They look much alike, although it appears to him that one is slightly smaller. Their skin is soft and delicate. He strokes their short, kinky, black hair. Even when they move on their cloth, they are quiet.

From his youth, he's known those who believed multiple births are a curse. Victoria, too, once had held that belief. But he's never understood why people fear twins. Have they seen twin goats or sheep? Do their babies differ from those of the animals? Is there evil in the goats or sheep? They aren't destroyed. How curious is fear that comes to the mind. Even terror when one sees something that isn't understood. Afraid of anything that is different from the accepted.

"Who can look at two such beautiful children and decide they must be destroyed? There is no evil here!" John whispers tenderly.

As he is kneeling beside the twins, Laraba awakens. She looks through the doorway. She sees a man near her babies. She shivers. Then she remembers where she is and recognizes John.

She arises and goes into the room where he is gazing at her babies. When he sees Laraba's frowning face, he welcomes her to his home. He encourages her not to worry.

"Victoria has told me about your coming and your concern. You may stay with us as long as you need to."

"Thank you, thank you!" bursts from Laraba's lips, as tears fill her eyes. "I cannot thank you enough!"

"Laraba, how did you gain the strength to search for the babies?"

"I do not know, but I wanted them. I knew I should not look for them. But I had to find my babies. I was terrified that something would happen before I found them."

"Are you not afraid to keep the babies?"

"Yes, even now I shudder when I think about what I have done. But I would do it again."

Soon John excuses himself. He goes to his room to rest a few hours. Before sleep overtakes him, he hears his brothers leaving for school. He knows when Victoria leaves, going to sell her fruit in the market.

Waking up, he tries to study, but he continues to ponder the customary beliefs about twins. In the late afternoon, Victoria returns to give John some food. Then it is time for him to go to work again. He dresses in a heavy coat and a warm scarf. He takes his torchlight with him to the compound where his employer lives.

◆　◆　◆　◆　◆

John guards a large, cement block house with many rooms and a cooking area inside the building. This home has domestic quarters. Those and several other buildings are enclosed with a high concrete fence. Broken bottles have been implanted along the top to prevent thieves from climbing over the wall. The Muslim master of this house has four wives and many children.

Some wine-colored bougainvillea bushes are near the gate. Geraniums with blooming red clusters planted in pots sit along the walkway. A frangipani tree adds more color. Also there are small orange and banana trees in the back yard. The mango tree on the side of the house is larger than the guava tree nearby. John is allowed to pick as much fruit as he wants to eat. Sometimes one of the madams of the house tells him to take fruit home to his family.

Reaching that compound in the Government Reservation Unit (GRU), he sees an empty wooden packing crate. It had been discarded by the owner. He breaks it open. With its pieces he builds a small fire in the back of the house. This feels good, as the night is cool. The glow of the fire attracts insects and Ali, the night watchman for another house within the same enclosure.

Ali and John are friends. Nightly between rounds, after the doors and windows are checked, they talk first at one place then the other. Ali is powerfully built; strong hands hold his Islamic prayer beads. He approaches John. This night he slips the beads into his pocket.

"How is your house?" John questions.

"All is well."

"What is the news?"

"I know none. And what do you know?"

"Last night while the crickets sang, one came to my house with twins. There is much life in my house now."

Ali isn't surprised at John's tone and manner. These words from some men would bring apprehension and misgivings. But this isn't true when they come from John. Often they talk about God. They don't agree, but they deeply and sincerely respect each other.

"Yes," continues John. "One Laraba from Barikin Biyu brought them to our house. Audu, her husband, had taken them to the forbidden bush to die. But she recovered them and brought them here."

"It is strange—the part of a person that would believe twins to be evil. But some do. They think them like animals which are born several at a time," comments Ali. "And they believe people cannot be like animals. So, if more than one is born at one time, it is evil. They think it will bring disaster to the compound and village."

"Yes, but I think fear and not knowing better are the causes for these beliefs. I do not think it is because of hate. Such terror comes from ignorance. Often we despise what we do not understand. What is different seems dangerous."

"You are right. That is so. But we also scoff at what we cannot control. That is the work of Allah. He is over everything. He determines whether there will be one or two, male or female. We do not like it. That's because we are bound by something over which we have no say," answers Ali.

"The man who will destroy his own will rejoice when his heifer bears two calves. He is not surprised or perplexed when his nanny goat has twin kids. But let his wife or the wife of another give birth to two and his first thought is that they are evil." John shakes his head.

"Yes, and let us remember that many see a birth as the return of one who has deceased. When twins are born, it can only mean that two from the deceased family are fighting to return. If both come together, there will be trouble for the family. Only one can successfully return at a time," Ali reminds John.

"True, many believe this because it is the only way they can deal with their grief when a loved one dies. The return of the deceased by a later birth gives them a measure of peace," remarks John thoughtfully.

"Perhaps one could argue this justifies such a belief."

John stands. He tears another board from the box. It's added to the fire. As it blazes, an insect whirls itself into the flames. Its wings burn as it falls to death in the fire.

"There is much we do not know. But to say we fear all that we do not understand is not so," warns John.

"That is true. Fear does come through ignorance. However, we do not dread all that we are unable to understand. We only fear the unknown that touches us."

"Then we agree."

"Let's talk some more when I return. Now I must see about the place."

Ali leaves the circle of light. He goes into the darkness. Gathering his cloth about himself, he wants to preserve some of the warmth. He makes his regular route around the house he guards, as John circles the house he watches.

Upon returning to the fire, Ali asks, "Why did this woman recover the twins? It is not what one would expect."

"No, it is not done. I have asked her that same question."

"What was her answer?"

"Her answer was short in words, but long in meaning. It was significant. 'I wanted them,' she pointed out. 'My need for them was great. I could not control my going.'"

"Aah, aah, it is different," responds Ali, clicking his tongue.

"She went on to tell me that she would do it again."

"Is she of a rebellious spirit?"

"No, I have not found her so."

"This thing she did is strange."

"Well, it is unusual. But I am glad she did it."

"Yes, what she did is good. Now what will happen? Who will care for them?"

"It will be difficult, but it can be done."

"Will her husband come?"

"I do not know Audu. So I do not know what he will do."

"Does he know where she is?"

"No. She has not told anyone where she is."

"It will be hard for him to find her."

"Yes, unless she wants him to."

"It is difficult for me to understand her actions. I would think fear of the babies would have stopped her."

"She does not seem to be afraid of them. She is a strong woman."

"Why? Do not all of her people believe the birth of two is evil?"

"I do not know. She found them and brought them to Victoria and me. We only met Laraba one time before. Still, we became friends then. She said she could think of no other place to go where she felt they would all be safe."

CHAPTER ELEVEN

Trip to Danbar

One evening, as Audu walks home from his market stall, he hoarsely whispers to himself, "I must go to Danbar. They could be there. I may not be able to find them. Still I must go there to look for them."

When he reaches his compound, he tells Uwa, "I am going to Danbar. That may be where Laraba took the two. She must be there. I can think of no other place to search."

"Danbar is a wicked place. All are strangers there. If she is there, how will you find her?"

"I do not know. But I must go. The shadows have reached their longest lengths. It is too late to start today. I will leave tomorrow."

"Who do you know who lives there?"

"There are several. Remember, Sidi went to Danbar many years ago. When he visited here last year he told me he liked the town," pronounces Audu.

Uwa shrugs her shoulders, "I fear you going there."

"I will be all right," Audu assures her.

That night Audu joins the other men sitting beside the large tree on the edge of the village. They gather to drink palm wine and beer. He arrives later than the others. He carefully slips over to one side and sits a short distance from the group. He hopes he'll not be noticed. They might make him leave or say harsh things about him and his family. Soon most of them are drunk. All speak in loud voices. Many talk at the same time. A fellow comes over to the rock where he is sitting. Audu doesn't recognize him.

"Has your wife returned?" the man asks in a slurred tone. "I saw her with the two devils running wild and scared."

Audu's eyes flash with interest and anger. "Where did you see her?"

"My throat is dry. I cannot speak again."

"Here, take this to wet your throat," Audu says as he hands him a small bottle of beer. "But before you go, tell me where you saw her."

"On the big road going towards Danbar. I do not know why the driver stopped and agreed to take her with him. But I too could see that she is good and to be desired." The man grins lustfully and rolls his eyes. He winks at those nearby.

Filled with anger and worry, Audu strikes the man across his face with a flat hand. Then he marches away from the drinking place. On the way home, he hears women singing and drummers drumming. Over and over the rhythm of the drums and the voices echo through the darkness, "She is good and to be desired." These words resound in his mind as he unrolls his sleeping mat to prepare for the night. Tears cloud his eyes. Apprehension fills his heart as he thinks about Laraba.

"Oh, Laraba, Laraba, where are you? Are you safe?" he moans into the night.

There are many insects. Despite the heat, Audu wraps himself in his sleeping cloth. He seeks some feeling of security. Terrible dreams invade his sleep. He fights one away. Another comes to take its place. He sees Laraba in the city and strains to drive away the thoughts of what could happen to her there. It is a night of torture. It's another like many he has had since she left him. The long days without her are terrible, but the nights are far worse. When the cock heralds the morning, he is tired and weary. But he's glad daylight has come.

Audu arises from his mat. He opens his door to what appears to be a bright, sunny day. Stretching to his fullest height, he goes to fill a calabash with water. With this he washes his face and neck. The cool water feels good. He moves towards the place of the fire. Uwa is already there. Smelling the bubbling porridge, he realizes that he is hungry. For the first time in many days, he wants food.

"Food will be ready soon. I knew you would want to leave early," his mother says.

After eating, Audu returns to his hut. He finds his small wooden box. Several pieces of clothing are put in it. Then he reaches into the bottom of his large clothes container. A little, ragged sack of rough material is removed. Inside is the money he has saved. This was for his expected son's school fees and other things the boy would need. But he expects food and lodging will cost much in Danbar. So he takes out many of the coins and most of the notes he thinks he'll need to pay his way in the city. These funds are placed in a deep pocket within his long, flowing robe. Quickly, he shoves the bag containing the rest of his money back to leave in his hut. Audu also takes a few important papers he may need.

Uwa had wrapped some died meat and pounded yams in fresh banana leaves. After placing these in his box, he locks it and puts the key with his pocketed money.

As Audu turns to leave, he notices his bright yellow bird. Remembering the many happy hours its songs had provided, he decides to take him along. With the box on his head and the birdcage in one hand, he bids his mother goodbye. He quickens his pace to the motor park. He hopes to find a lorry going to Danbar. Although he is anxious about going to the big city, he is eager to get there and look for Laraba.

There are three lorries in the park. All are being loaded with bags of guinea corn, millet and maize from the early-producing farms. There are also boxes with unmarked contents. Each lorry has an inscription over the cab. "God's Case—No Appeal" is on the pale black one. On another it states, "The Big Leaf shall not Crush the Small." Finally Audu comes to a faded green vehicle going to Danbar with "No Condition Is Permanent" as its motto. On top of the goods being transported is room for passengers to sit.

Others are waiting to ride in the lorry. Audu questions them about the cost of their trip. Then he looks for the driver's helper. He finds the man asleep on a hammock beneath his old vehicle. After agreeing on the fare, Audu pays the price. He takes his seat by the window in the front. When there are enough goods and the required number of passengers to make it financially worthwhile, the trip begins. The motor is started. It rattles out of the park and down the bumpy dirt road. The driver, Audu, and one other passenger sit in the cab. Most of the others traveling with them are from surrounding villages. Some are traders from distant places.

A few hours after they had started the trip, the vehicle shakes and veers to the right. It is a struggle to bring it back in place.

"Chi, chi, what is wrong?" mutters the owner.

Then he realizes it's a flat tire. The lorry is safely brought to a stop and stays on the road. It'll be easier to change the tire here. Besides, who can tell what the side of the road is like? There might be stones that would be hard on the other tires, or he might get stuck there. Quickly the driver's helper swings down from the back of the lorry. He takes a block of wood with its convenient handle and puts it under the left rear tire.

The driver moves out to the other side. He and his assistant go into the bush on each side of the road. They begin breaking branches from the trees. These are placed along the road several hundred feet in both directions. This warns approaching vehicles that a motor is parked on the road.

Audu opens the door and steps out into the sunshine. Passengers who have been sitting on bags or boxes climb down from the back of the vehicle. As they descend, some complain about the difficult ride. They don't like the delay this stop is causing. Others get down quietly. Legs hurt as they touch the ground. They are stiff and cramped from sitting in one position. Audu takes the birdcage from the back of the lorry and places it carefully on his seat in the cab. He looks to see if it has food and water and decides his canary will be fine until they get to the city.

They stopped not far from a few family huts. Some of the passengers walk towards them in search of water and food. After Audu makes sure the bird is secure in its cage, he follows the others. He notices that this is a dirty, desolate place. Two fires seem to burn from habit; they receive little attention. A few swollen-bellied, naked children lifelessly kick a small rubber ball. Men sit quietly in the shade of several scrub trees. They are eating ears of hard corn that have been roasted over an open fire. The women wait in the doors of their dark huts.

"Can we take water?" one man asks, as he strolls towards the well.

"You can," one in the shade answers. "Bring the bucket," he calls out.

One of the larger boys leaves his game. He moves quickly towards a hut. Soon he returns with a bucket attached to a long, much-used rope. The riders walk over to the well beside the huts. It is deep, made even deeper by the days without rain. The bucket hits the water.

It's tipped to fill. Hand over hand, the rope is drawn. Spilling water splashes as it returns to its source. The water is shared with those from the lorry. All drink out of the same cup. The bucket, rope and two pennies are handed to the boy. He runs back to the huts with them. Those in the shade don't speak.

The usual small table with its stacks of goods for sale isn't evident beside the road. Sensing that nothing more is to be gained in this place, the group of travelers turn around. They walk towards the lorry. To get away from the sun and to rest, each seeks a place under the nearby trees. They sit or stretch out for a nap or to talk.

Audu goes to the truck. He opens his box and takes out some of the food Uwa had prepared for him. He eats.

It doesn't take long to change the wheel, since they don't bother to repair the tire and tube.

The driver calls, "We are ready to go."

When his passengers have all boarded the lorry, he starts the sputtering engine. The helper pulls the wooden block from under the wheel and pushes it through the rectangular hole in the tailgate. The motor begins to move slowly forward. He hurriedly climbs up the back of the lorry over the tailgate, and takes his place near the cab. Finally, the lorry eases down the road, and their trip continues.

Audu watches the road ahead. He notices the land is not as good as his. Farms are not neat. Trees are just scrub. People suffer. Not enough to sell. Not enough to eat. *Why do they stay?*

The little bird hops around in his cage, irritated by the fumes and the noises. Even so, Audu is pleased he brought him along. He is glad the bird is in front. However, this makes it uncomfortable. But the latch isn't strong. He won't get out of his cage. Might have in the back.

A man, two women, and a goat stand beside the road. The man waves his hands, trying to attract the attention of the lorry owner, who keeps his eyes on the road. He acts as if he doesn't see them. Conversation among the three strangers in the cab has been exhausted. Each now follows his own thoughts. It is then that Audu realizes how foolish he has been.

He remembers he left home in a thoughtless way. He forgot to get the names and addresses of fellow villagers in Danbar. He's positive Sidi is there. He seemed to have been making a prosperous living.

How could he have forgotten a friend from childhood? Others are there. Surely he'll be able to find some brother in the city.

After they cross the bridge and approach a small village, Audu watches as a mother duck and her ducklings waddle across the road in single file. The speed is reduced in order to swerve around them. To hit them would be dangerous. Ducks and sheep are the only things on the road one must not run over. Goats, dogs, and people aren't extended the same courtesy. They must fend for themselves.

After the excitement of the last few miles, the trip becomes tedious again. They travel along undisturbed. Audu's mind turns to his family, especially his brother. Bala is no longer in Danbar. But he had told many things about life there. He hopes he has enough money. The lorry fair was not too much. He questions how much food will cost until he finds someone he knows. He didn't want to take too much from his savings. Surely he'll soon find a fellow tribesman, a brother, who will help him.

Audu is abruptly brought back to the present. The motor begins its descent toward a long, narrow bridge. From the opposite direction comes a heavily-loaded, red mammy wagon. There is not room for the two vehicles to pass. It appears that neither driver intends to stop. Audu is sure that the two are going to crash into each other.

He stiffens, grabs his bird cage, and shouts, "Are you not going to stop?"

"Let him wait," the somber voice replies.

"He will not and the two cannot pass!"

Just at the last moment, Audu's driver pulls to the side. He safely stops a few feet from the bridge buttress. A red streak thunders past in a cloud of dust. Audu and his companions on the front seat can see the grinning face of the man behind the other wheel. He has won. Audu's driver shrugs and curses his triumphant opponent as the flash of red passes by.

For several miles, all they see is the narrow road. The sparse woods on either side have a few monkeys in the trees. Tired and deep in thought, Audu jumps, startled by the ringing of a small bell near his head. The bell signals that another motor is coming up from the rear. Because of their own noisy engine, Audu doesn't hear the honking of the horn behind them. He's sure that it sounded, because their driver is in the middle of the road, he must not have noticed it either. However, it's customary for someone to stand up in the back, so they can watch for anyone wanting to pass. If a person is not allowed to pass, it might be seen as a barricade.

As soon as the advancing vehicle gets close, the watchman climbs over the bags of goods. He pulls several times on the string connected to the bell in the cab. When the vehicle moves over, he turns to motion that it is safe to pass. The approaching lorry roars around them and speeds on its way.

As they reach the top of the next hill, the man behind the wheel applies the brakes. In front of them, they see a road block. It's made with a few large, black, metal drums. Some soldiers, with guns on their shoulders, are walking around a lorry already parked there. It's the one that had just passed them. Everyone has gotten out and is standing beside their motor. Curious, yet afraid to intrude, the owner of Audu's lorry waits to see what is going to happen.

"What does it mean?" asks Audu.

"Who can know?"

They roll to a stop. Three soldiers, holding their rifles pointed toward the sky, walk up to the door on the right side. One of them commands, "Everyone come down!"

Those inside the cab step out. The others in the back begin to slip down to the ground. One soldier gruffly states, "Driver, show me your licenses and those of your vehicle. I am to inspect them." After carefully examining them, he hands the papers back.

A corporal moves from passenger to passenger. He repeats the same questions over and over, "What is your name? Where are you going? Why?"

He approaches Audu and asks, "What is your name?"

"Audu."

"Where are you going?"

"To Danbar."

"For what purpose?"

With his heart racing and hands beginning to sweat, Audu can't answer. He fears telling that he's looking for his wife and the twins, who had disappeared. So, he quickly replies, "To buy goods for trading."

Another armed man climbs up on the sacks and boxes of goods. He thrusts his bayonet into a bag. The contents of guinea corn falls to the floor.

Pointing to a box, the soldier asks, "Whose box is this?"

Hesitantly one of the men steps forward.

"Open it!"

With a small key, he opens the lock. He removes the hasp. The box contains only a few carpenter's tools—a hammer, a saw, a pincer, and a measuring tape.

Without comment, the searcher moves to another box. "Someone come and open this one," he demands.

A young girl climbs up to open it. Rummaging through the clothing inside, the soldier finds nothing of interest to him.

The sergeant calls the owner aside. They walk away from the group to talk. Others may not have noticed, but Audu sees his driver pass some money to the man. It's clear to him that the soldiers have adopted the methods of the police. They require a bribe for any service rendered or to prevent a problem from arising.

In a few minutes, orders are given, "You can get back in the lorry and leave."

The sergeant commands a soldier to remove the barricade. He motions them to move on. Soon, the lorry is far down the road. When the soldiers can't hear them, they all begin to speak at once.

"What does this mean?" Audu asks again.

"Who can tell?" the driver answers in a low and unsteady voice.

The other passenger in the front seat states with hesitation, "Two days ago some soldiers stopped another lorry I was traveling in. They searched everyone and everything."

"What did they want?"

"I do not know. But I have heard they are in many places, even in some townships."

"Why?"

"I do not know that either. But it makes me afraid. I drive this lorry many miles. I do not need to be stopped," he mumbles, but says no more.

Audu realizes the man remembers he is sharing his cab with two men he doesn't know. He doesn't want to discuss the matter any further. He feels sure the owner will investigate the matter more with his own people when he returns home.

Then the owner sternly adds, "We must not guess what is going to happen."

Soon, they see shops and homes in the distance. As they enter Danbar, they notice there are only a few people on the streets. Although this means little to Audu, it brings fear to those who are familiar with the city. This area is always filled with many people. One must continually blow the horn to clear the street for passage. Because the three sitting in the cab are strangers to each other, little is said. But all eyes examine the streets and wonder about its desertion. Farther on, they see a crowd filling the streets. A few blocks away, a group of men is attacking a man. It is growing dark. To avoid the possibility of trouble or a riot, the driver turns down another road.

"I am glad he knows a different way to the lorry park," the man in the middle says, as he squints his eyes.

As soon as they stop in the motor park, Audu climbs down. Carefully, he places the cage holding his canary on the ground. Then he reaches back into the cab for his box. It had been riding at his feet. He's tired and dirty even though he has ridden in the cab.

"Where do I go now?" he asks, speaking to no one.

Many of those in the back of the lorry put their loads on their heads. They move towards the gate of the park. Some hire men to take their things for them. The items are placed on the carriers' heads, and they follow the owners away. Others stand, as Audu does, not knowing where to go.

A taxi driver calls out, "Come, ride with me! I can take you to where you want to go. It will be a cheap, cheap ride."

"Come with me. I have a place to go," entreats a young girl. She stands next to where the lorry is parked. She is homely. Evidently, she's not gifted in her trade.

Without answering, Audu turns. He starts walking toward the gate. He's not accustomed to sitting cramped up for a long period of time, so he moves haltingly. His legs are sore. Two police officers with rifles stand nearby watching the street. Going only a few hundred yards, Audu stands in front of the Jolly Hotel. He enters the dimly-lit lobby. It's tiny and dingy. Two men sit inside on stools, talking in subdued voices.

CHAPTER TWELVE

A Strange Place

I would like a room for the night." Audu speaks in an anxious yet controlled tone.

One of the men stands and beckons him to follow. He leads Audu out into a small courtyard. The other man follows carrying a lamp. Taking his keys from his pocket, the first man opens one of the doors facing a treeless yard. Both men frown. They seem nervous and uncertain as they examine Audu. They stare at his tribal marks trying to determine who he is.

The open door reveals a small room with only one window. When the man presses the switch beside the door, a single light bulb hanging from the ceiling gives light to the room. The only furnishings are a bamboo bed with a straw-filled mattress and a low bench. The lamp is placed on the bench.

"How much is the rent?" Audu asks wearily.

"One shilling for the night."

Because he's tired and gripped with an uneasy feeling, Audu doesn't argue, but gives the money to the one who had opened the door.

As he takes the money, the man says, "Allah give you rest and wake you well."

"Thank you, and may you two rest well," the weary traveler responds.

One of the men picks up the lamp. The two leave, closing the door behind them. Audu slides the bolt, securely locking the door.

"Whew!" He sighs. "I am glad those men did not ask questions that I cannot answer."

Stooping down, he opens his box. First, he removes some of the leftover yam and dried meat. Hungrily, he eats part of the food and prepares for bed. His body feels heavy and weary from the long, difficult trip. His mental anguish increases the physical exhaustion that overcomes him. Those longest days in the market, even with all their difficulties, never made him as weary as he is at the end of this journey. But he is glad he is here.

◆　◆　◆　◆　◆

Not being used to sleeping on a bed and being in this strange place, he will not rest well. Sleep doesn't come immediately, despite his weariness. A mosquito hums. His thoughts turn to night at home with its many sounds. He remembers the chopping of firewood by those who return late from the farm. A donkey braying as if laughing at them for being late. The steady rhythm of the pestle in the mortar prepares the grain for the pot. The crackling fire. The rattling of metal pots and pans. The squawking chickens roosting unsteadily on the limbs of the trees. Dogs barking at those returning from the market or those making a last trip to the stream. Bats and night birds add to the noise with their cries and wings beating in their quest for food. And there are the human sounds. A crying child impatiently waiting to be fed. A tired, angry wife or a drunken man becoming boisterous. A young drummer eager for the night of singing and dancing to begin. A cyclist ringing his bell to announce his return, and night time greetings from friend to friend. How many sounds there are to enjoy! Oh, how he misses those familiar sounds on this night as he imagines them and the comfort they so often bring. He thinks night has also begun in his village.

Now the strange noises of the city replace those pleasant and tranquil remembrances. He hears the ringing of too many bicycle bells and loud talk in languages he doesn't understand. Many feet walk near his room. The honking vehicle horns are never heard at home. All bring concern. *What's happening outside this compound?* During the brief moments when the noises abate, the silence adds even more to his anxiety.

The deep longings for home and Laraba delay his sleep. What will he do when daylight appears? Audu's mind is as restless as his body. Thoughts rush through his feverish brain. It's like a never-ending waterfall or the rapids of a swollen river. He can't focus on any one thing long enough to uncover its meaning. At last, sleep captures him, though he is unaware of when or how.

Sometime very early in the morning, Audu awakens. It's before daylight. He feels uncomfortable and disoriented after disturbed sleep. Soon, he remembers where he is and why he is here. He tosses and turns, waiting for the sun long before it peeps over the trees. His uneasiness only seems to delay it. He remains on his bed a few minutes after he sees light through the cracks in the wooden window he had carefully locked before going to bed. After dressing, he slides back the bolt and opens the door to a deserted yard. He visits the latrine in the corner of the compound. Moving to the faucet, he draws water. It's cool and refreshing to his face and neck. Returning to his room, he folds the sleeping cloth. That he puts it into his box with yesterday's clothing. Then he eats the remaining yam and dried meat Uwa had prepared for him. Taking his box and birdcage, he leaves the room.

As Audu goes out of the hotel, he pauses to speak to a man standing by the door, "Good morning." Then, not waiting for the customary response, he continues, "Please give me directions to the central market."

Recognizing he is speaking to a stranger, the man replies, "It is not far from here. Do you know the location of the motor park?"

"Yes, I do."

"It is only a short distance on the other side of the park."

"Thank you very much." Audu hastens off into the early morning light. He thinks perhaps he'll soon find someone from his village. They'll help him. His face brightens at the prospect of some word about Laraba.

Many are going to the market. They carry head loads of various sizes and shapes. A woman walks along, balancing a large net filled with plastic vessels in bright colors of red, yellow and green. Another has a big metal bowl containing ripe orange-colored mangoes to sell. A man has a pile of locally-woven blue, white, and black cloth stacked on his head. He is followed by a young boy with a basket of squawking chickens to be sold alive. Running toward him is a boy selling newspapers. He holds a paper up for Audu to see, calling out, "Buy my newspaper. Learn the news."

The bold black headline "ARMY TAKE OVER" jumps out at Audu. "I will buy your paper," he declares. Taking three pence from his pocket, he pays for the paper.

Putting the birdcage and his box on the ground, he sits on the box and reads. His eyes widen in astonishment at the words. It says that some soldiers had killed several army officers and government leaders and imprisoned others. The army had taken over the affairs of the government. Audu ponders this information a few moments. He wonders what it all means.

"This will not change my purpose for coming to Danbar," he whispers to himself. "I must find Laraba quickly so I can take her back home!" Folding the paper, he puts it in the large pocket of his regalia. It's one of his best garments. The white material has white embroidery around the neck and on the sleeves. He walks on down the street.

As Audu enters the Danbar market, he can't believe what he sees. There are stalls everywhere. People, noise, and clanging cycle bells are seen and heard in every direction. One area is provided for the tailors. They sit on the ground. With their right hands, they turn the wheels of their sewing machines, guiding the cloth with their left. He stops long enough in the men's clothes section to see the golden design a man is making around the neck of a blue garment. Not far away are cloth sellers. There are many stalls of different kinds of material. Any color one wants can be found here. Some are imported. Others are woven in the area and sewn together in about 8-inch wide strips.

Of course, he notices the booths with the blue, white, red, yellow, and green tie-dye cloth, like those worn by many women in his village. This all brings to his mind his interest and efforts of purchasing cloth for the expected son. It also causes a frown to crease his forehead. Uneasiness tightens his stomach. He stands transfixed, staring off into space. Briefly, he forgets to examine every face for tribal marks like his own. His mind is busy replaying the night the two were born. But reality returns when someone bumps into him. He reaches up to catch and steady the box on his head.

Audu continues his move in the market, inspecting people as he goes. He sees the area filled with sewing thread, yarn, buttons, and other items needed to make clothes. Next, he sees the brilliantly colored red, green, blue, and white beads shipped from England, as well as others made locally. They are hanging across the booths, displaying their beauty to attract buyers. All the while, Audu gives superficial attention to these things. He is intent on his search.

Progressing through the market, he comes to the pottery section. It has clay pots in many different sizes and shapes that have been baked to the needed hardness. He recognizes those used for cooking, holding water, soap-making, dyeing, and other purposes. Some are like those at home used by Laraba, Uwa, and the other women.

Nearby he sees tools for farming, things like short-handled hoes, cutlasses, and machetes, along with hardware for other needs. Furniture items are together in another place.

Hour after hour, Audu slowly walks through the market and the streets bordering it, but to no avail. His countenance crumples with despair. His head begins to pound. Aloud, he whispers, "What am I to do? I have spent hours roaming this market full of people. Somewhere among them there must be someone from my people—someone who can help me."

He trudges along, looking for a place to sit and rest. The box he balances on his head has become heavy. Often he reaches up to hold it in place. His neck is tired from having to move around to dodge being jostled by the crowd. His hand is sore from tightly gripping the bird cage handle so it will not be knocked to the ground. A little farther on, he comes to the edge of the market. He lowers his cage and puts his box down, then wearily sits upon the box. Knotting his hands into tight fists, he plants his elbows on his legs near his knees, bending over to put his chin in his hands. Closing his eyes, he feels their wetness. He must not allow the tears to flow; he doesn't want to show his great emotions. His mind takes him back home and to the bewitched twins. He wonders about them. *Have they been destroyed?*

"Yes, they are the reason life has become so difficult. They must be blinding me from finding a brother here. What has become of them?"

The bird was quiet while Audu roamed from stall to stall. Now it bursts forth in song. Opening his eyes, Audu lifts his face. He smiles at his beautiful yellow bird.

"I am glad I brought you with me," he whispers.

After a brief rest, Audu returns to the main market. There are hundreds of busy people here. But some stand around doing nothing.

Many came to the city with a purpose. Others drifted here aimlessly. And now there are many with nothing to do.

Passing an eating place that he had not noticed earlier in the day, he stops and sits on a bench. Only one kind of food is available. The woman cooking and selling doesn't speak. But she gets a bowl of rice with three or four small pieces of meat on top. From the pan she takes a large spoon and covers the food with rich red gravy. She places it before him.

"How much?"

"One shilling."

Audu hands her the money. She leaves to serve another.

While he is eating, a tall, lean man comes and sits beside him. The man places his elbows on the table. He buries his face in his hands. Audu notices they are strong hands, accustomed to heavy toil. The stranger doesn't look up until he hears the bowl placed on the table. Without speaking, he hands the woman some money. Picking up the spoon, he aimlessly stirs the food with little enthusiasm.

After he has eaten a few spoonfuls, Audu comments to him, "The food is good."

"Yes, it is good." His eyes light up, showing his surprise that someone has spoken to him.

Audu observes his bright eyes and the long, thin tribal marks on his face. The two eat without further words. After finishing, Audu remains sitting at the table. He hopes the man will talk with him. He wants some conversation now. This person seems a likely prospect. But he takes the last piece of meat from the bowl. While still chewing it, he stands up and walks away. After the man leaves, Audu turns to face the market. Still, he remains seated on the bench alone and lonely. A girl passes by, selling oranges. Audu selects two and hands her one pence. He peels one and begins eating it. He looks up, surprised to see the tall man returning to the table.

"I just realized you must be new to the city."

"Yes, how did you know?"

"Your box. One who lives here would not bring a box to the market."

"Yes, I have come from Barikin Biyu. I hope to find someone from home. So far I have not been successful."

"I do not know anyone from there, but I have a friend in the market. He might be able to help you. Come, let us go and see," encourages the man.

"Good."

Without hesitation, Audu gets up. He places his box on his head and takes his birdcage by the wire handle, and he follows the man. As they walk between the stalls and pass many shoppers, Audu searches each face intently. If only he could find Laraba, he is sure they could come to some understanding. He didn't mean to hurt her, only to do what was necessary. Everything happened so quickly. There wasn't time to think or to talk together.

As they hurry on, they pass a man ringing a bell to attract attention to his assorted used clothing. The most attractive apparel has been placed on top of the various piles.

Then Audu and his new friend stop on Hospital Road. They study a drama unfolding before their eyes. A half-naked, dirty, deranged woman with matted hair sits by the roadside. She furiously beats two discarded, red and white, bent and holey enamel bowls like they were drums. Most of those who pass by ignore her. A dapper young man carrying a briefcase hastens past in front of her. Suddenly, the woman drops her enamel bowls. She gets up and reaches her filthy arms and hands toward him. The startled man cries out. He runs from her as fast as his legs will carry him. The woman, seeing she can't catch him, returns to her place on the ground and goes back to frantically beating her bowls.

Audu and the stranger skirt three unattended, empty pushcarts. They continue on their way. Soon they come to a place where three young, professional letter writers are busy. The men are helping two older men and a woman.

"In a moment, my friend will finish the letter he is writing. Then we will ask about someone from your place. Many come to him for help. He is an educated man. He can write in four languages."

While they wait, Audu notices a sugarcane seller nearby. She has chewed much of her cane. The remains lie on the ground in front of her. He hopes to be more successful than this woman.

He also sees a blind beggar sitting on the ground nearby. He's not even bothering to call for alms.

The woman pays the letter-writer, who is sitting on a stool behind a small wooden table. She thanks him for his work. With letter in hand, she leaves to go to the post office where she will purchase a stamp to mail her letter.

"Friday, I want you to meet my friend. He has come looking for someone from his village."

"Welcome, welcome," the young man responds pleasantly.

"Thank you. How is your work?"

"Work is fine. Many need letters and papers written. May I write a letter for you?"

"No, I am trying to find someone from Barakin Biyu. Can you help me?"

"Let me think." He hesitates a moment, "No, I do not believe I know anyone from there, but I have written letters to that place." Turning to his associates, he asks, "Do either of you know anyone from there? My friend is looking for someone from his town."

As Audu and the men talk, another man walks up. He stops and listens. Soon, he too enters the conversation. Turning to Audu he asks, "Where are you from?"

"Barikin Biyu."

"Barikin Biyu?" he questions.

"Yes," replies Audu, noting from the many short, broad tribal marks that this stranger is of another people group. Yet Audu hopes he might know someone from his area or at least someone from his people.

"Why would one come to this large town without the names and addresses of his brothers?" he asks loudly. Clicking his tongue with contempt, he adds, "That must be a bush place for one to act like this!"

"It is not bush! You are showing your own ignorance by such talk!" Audu exclaims, forgetting for a moment his own problem. He speaks in defense of his people.

The stranger shakes his head and laughs. Speaking to the men sitting and standing around, he asks, "Would one of you do such a foolish thing?"

"Of course not!" Friday answers with indignation. Then he sees Audu's frowning-face. He realizes that he might be a future customer. He adds, "But perhaps this man has a reason for such behavior, though I can think of none."

Clicking his tongue again, the stranger strolls away. He indicates to all who can hear his loud voice that he couldn't understand the stupidity of some people.

Friday turns to Audu and says, "That man is from Kobana. Do not let him trouble you. There are none as backward as his people. I daresay most of the stealing done in this very market is done by his brothers."

Audu, remembering his purpose for questioning these men, reminds the others, "You did not say if you know anyone from my village."

"Now I remember. I believe that Mai-zane, the cloth seller, is from there. Several times I have written letters for him to that place. If you would like, I will lead you to his stall. Perhaps he can help you."

"Thank you, I would appreciate that very much," Audu smiles.

He chuckles with excitement. Perhaps Mai-zane can help. Audu thanks the man who had brought him to the letter-writers and the others. His heart beats faster as Friday leaves his table. He follows the letter writer. They hurry through the market toward the stall of the cloth seller. They pass through much of the same area that Audu had traveled earlier that day. The blind beggar remains in silence. The deranged one stills beats upon her bowls.

"It is not far, we will soon be there."

When they arrive, the stall is closed. The tin door is securely locked. "Where is Mai-zane?" Friday asks the man in the next stall.

"He is not here. He did not come to the market today."

"Where may we find him?"

"I do not know. I have cloth. Is that what you want? Come, come look at this." He holds up a brightly colored yellow and red piece of cloth.

"No, we want Mai-zane. My friend is looking for someone from his village."

"I cannot help. Come tomorrow. Perhaps he will return."

Audu's shoulders droop. His voice breaks with disappointment as he asks, "Do you know where he lives?"

"No. I do not."

"Then we will go. Thank you."

Again thanking Friday for his help, Audu starts off in another direction, but then he sees a man that reminds him of Sidi. Hope wells up as he calls, "Sidi. Sidi." There is no response. Before Audu can catch him, the man disappears in the market.

CHAPTER THIRTEEN

Danger

At first, Laraba is uncertain about leaving the compound of John and Victoria. She is unfamiliar with the town and the people living around them. But one day, Victoria suggests she go to the fruit stands near the main market to purchase some plantains for them to fry. After several days of coaxing, Laraba ties her babies on. She starts down the dirt path. On the way, just as she turns a corner several blocks away, she notices smashed windows. The doors are broken in some of the houses. She sees that most buildings in this section of town have been destroyed or damaged. They are beyond repair. Some are on fire.

Quickly, Laraba slips back out of sight behind a vacant house. People are screaming. As she peeps around, she sees two men lugging someone out of a house. They are beating him with large sticks. He struggles to breathe, until he is silent. She draws back, putting her hands over her mouth. Three men begin breaking the windows of a car in a nearby yard. The shattering glass falls. She covers her ears. They slash the tires. The air oozes out. Next, they bash in the fenders and tops. The babies begin to stir. Laraba is afraid they will cry out. She rocks back and forth. Finally they go back to sleep. *Dare I try to go back to Victoria's?* She eases along the side of the house. Before reaching the back, she hears moaning not far away. She freezes in panic. For a few moments, everything is still. *What is happening?*

The leader of the pack calls out, "We are finished here. Let us go."

As the others follow, one tall man laughs and shouts, "We have been successful in ridding this town of our enemies."

Laraba squats down. She remains hidden. She listens to their loud talk and heavy steps. Finally, their sounds echo in the distance. Before turning to hurry back to John's house, she sneaks back to look out again. The backs of the group of men and boys are marching down the road in the distance. Thankfully, they are going in the opposite direction. Even though they are almost out of sight, she remains quiet. There are several dead bodies lying around on the ground. Nothing can be heard from the surrounding buildings.

Without making a sound, a young boy limps out of a house, dragging a bloody leg. He looks up and down the road. Seeing no one, he cries out in pain. He is followed by a woman crawling behind. One of her hands covers her slashed face. She shrieks out, "They killed my husband! Two of my children lie dead at my door. I am only alive because I pretended to be dead when they beat me. What will we do?"

Trembling violently, Laraba finds it hard to stand up. Bending over, she gags and vomits in the road. She stumbles over to lean against a tree. The babies start wiggling and begin to whine. Before she thinks to remove them, the one on her back wets her and her clothes, but she hardly notices. There is not enough strength in her arms to take it from her back. She hears the loud crying of the people around them. They seem to be wailing in the distance.

After a period of silence, someone calls out, "They have killed all the people in the house next to me. They beat them to death with their clubs. Who will they come after next? Where can we hide?"

The babies begin crying as loud as their tiny lungs will allow. She covers her mouth and turns around. With her head bent forward, she trots back down the road. Every few minutes, she reaches to gather a corner of her wrap to wipe her eyes.

Victoria hears loud shouts and runs outside of her house. She strains to see what is happening. She says to a neighbor, "I must go find Laraba. She did not want to go to the market, and I made her go. What if something happens to her?"

The friend walks out into the middle of the road. With one hand, she shades her eyes from the sun, trying to see who is approaching. She calls out, "I think I see her coming."

"I will never force her to leave this house again!" says Victoria, running to meet Laraba.

"Victoria, I am coming," sobs Laraba. "It is terrible, terrible! Do not go up this road. You do not need to see what is happening there."

"Thank God you are safe. Here, let me take one of the babies."

"Then we will go. Thank you."

CHAPTER FOURTEEN

A Place to Stay

Realizing that his hunt in Danbar might take a long time, Audu must find a place to stay. He leaves the market area and starts down one of the unpaved, rough roads. Remembering Friday's kindness, he quickly returns to his writing table.

"Friday, please, can you suggest a place for me to stay? A place that is not too dear."

"Since you do not have a brother to help you, I will try to think of some place. I am sorry, so sorry about your trouble. I certainly would want someone to help me if I should be alone and away from home. I hope you will find a brother soon."

"Thank you. It would be good if I could find a place not too far from here."

"I know a place. One that will suit you well."

"Where?"

"My brother, Taiwo, has a house on the third line from here."

"Same mother, same father?"

"No. But he is from my village. Taiwo has only one room to let."

"How much will it cost?"

"You will have to talk with him about that."

"What is the number?"

"It is 47/2 Block Street."

"How do you reach that place?"

"Go that way," replies Friday, pointing with his chin. "Go three poles and turn left. You will be on his line. Go until you find the number. It is plainly written on the wall beside the door."

"Thank you for your help. I hope we meet again."

"Perhaps we shall. Go well," admonishes Friday.

"Thank you. May you stay well."

Audu goes only a short distance. Then he is startled by the noise of a racing motor. Quickly he turns. An army jeep is coming at top speed. He jumps back from the side of the road, terrified. Hanging half out of the door-less vehicle is a reckless soldier with little driving ability. His left hand tightly grips the steering wheel; the other waves. No one knows what it means. It's evident to those walking on the road that the vehicle will not successfully make the round-about. The other men in his Land Rover don't seem to be aware of the impending danger, or they don't care. The nearer they come to the intersection, the faster they appear to go.

Seeing an old man cycling in the same direction, the people nearby watch in horror. They immediately know he neither sees nor hears the vehicle approaching because he stays in the road. If the soldiers fail to make the turn, the old man will be safe. But if they make it, the motor will hit him. Several call out.

"Get out of the way!"

"Make you leave the road."

It's too late. The old man's eyes open wide as he glances back. He can't get out of the way. The Land Rover's load of soldiers makes the turn at the very last moment, the result of luck, not skill. The cyclist is thrown out of the path of the vehicle and it passes over his bicycle. Sounds of the impact are clearly heard several blocks away. The jeep screeches to a stop a few hundred yards down the road. Followed by several other soldiers, the driver runs back to the old man, who sits on the road, surrounded by a crowd.

"Bush man! Bush man!" the driver screams. "Do you not know that we are the army? You are to get out of the way when we come!"

He raises his hand and hits the stricken man. The wounded man doesn't raise his hands or arms to ward off the angry blows, nor does he speak in his own defense. But he lifts his hands to cover his face.

"It is your fault. You should not have been on the road!"

An army officer observes the accident. Angered by the behavior of the soldiers, he hurries to help. "Leave the old man alone, you scoundrels! You will be charged."

When the soldiers hear his words of correction, they step back and crowd together. They all look at the ground, their faces deeply furrowed. They are surprised by his arrival, and now they are frightened by what he says. Though they might have thought of running away, none leave.

The spectators, who have been watching and grumbling, now come to the man's aid. They have been encouraged by the major's concern. Seeing there are several people to help him, Audu continues walking.

When he finds 47/2 Block Street, he places his box and cage on the ground. He claps his hands, calling out a greeting, "Hello, hello. Is anyone at home?"

An old woman comes to the door. Taken aback by her appearance, Audu stares at the sockets where eyes had once been. Hesitantly he says, "Friday directed me here. I understand there is a room to let."

The old woman responds with a soft and pleasant voice. "Yes, I will get my son." Moving to the door at the far end of the hall, she calls out, "Taiwo, Friday has sent one here!"

Without turning around, she speaks again, "Taiwo, come! A stranger is here."

A small, serious man comes out wiping his hands on a rag. "Welcome," he says, as he puts out his hands. "You are welcome."

"Thank you. How is this day for you?" Audu asks, responding to the outstretched hands.

"It is good. And how did you come?"

"Without trouble. Friday sent me. I have just come from his place in the market. Last night I arrived from home."

"You have come about the room?" When Audu nods, he says, "Come, I will show it to you."

"I have come with little money. How much is the room?"

"Come, look at it first. Then we will talk about the price."

The old woman moves from the entrance hall. She doesn't speak again. Audu notices that she doesn't feel with her hands but moves about without hesitation.

"Does your bird sing well?" the owner inquires, leading the way.

"Yes, he is one of the finest singers in our village."

"He is large and looks strong and bright," Taiwo comments as they reach the room. The door is closed but not locked. He leads Audu into the small room and goes over to open the only window for light. A wire and light socket hang from the ceiling.

"I will bring a globe," Taiwo states, as he quickly leaves and returns with a light bulb.

It is a plain room with few furnishings—a bed with a straw-filled mattress, a table, two chairs, and an earthen vessel. On one of the whitewashed walls, there is a faded picture of a former politician. It's like one of many photographs distributed by the government. The room is dingy but neat. Audu can tell it has been swept often.

"The room is nice?" asks Taiwo.

"Yes," Audu answers without enthusiasm. "How much is the rent?"

"Will you be here long?"

"It is impossible to know how long I will stay."

"The room is only one pound, five shillings a month."

"One pound, five!" says Audu in astonishment. "That is more than I can pay. If you will agree, I will give you fifteen shillings."

"You are a stranger here. Rooms are expensive. But since Friday sent you, I will let you have the room for one pound, three," Taiwo answers as he moves toward the door.

"The room costs more than I had thought, but I will give you eighteen shillings. I do this because Friday has been so kind and helpful."

"Very well," Taiwo sighs. "I will let you have it for one pound. That is my last price."

"Though that is much, I will agree."

"Good."

Audu puts his bird cage on a chair. He takes his box from his head. It feels good to be relieved of his loads. He pays for one week's rent. Taiwo hands him a key to the door and leaves. Audu looks around again at this small room. He hopes he'll not need it long. Since it's almost dark, he decides to feed his bird. He also gives it some water. Then he takes it outside. He looks around the neighborhood. He introduces himself to several who are lounging around. They are sitting on small wooden folding chairs or mats on the ground. Several ask him where is from. Others get up to look at his canary. Feeling weary, Audu soon returns to his room and goes to bed.

CHAPTER FIFTEEN

Audu and Yahaya Meet

Audu's chirping bird awakens him. It's time to begin a new day in the city far from home. He begins reflecting on what has happened. He thinks how long it's been since that night! But time doesn't really matter. He yearns to find Laraba. He questions whether she is here or some other place. He must get up and look more diligently.

The sun is bright. The sky is clear. The air is still as Audu peers through the tiny window. Quickly, he showers in the small building at the back of the house. After dressing, he locks his door and leaves his room. Going through the empty entrance hall, he approaches the street. He hasn't planned his day but knows he'll visit the cloth seller's stall. He isn't sure where else he will look today. After the night's rest, his steps are brisk and his eyes bright. Many people are on their way to work. The streets are crowded with cyclists and pedestrians moving like an outgoing wave. They are determined and move swiftly. Many are crowded together when Audu reaches the corner.

"Has there been an accident?" he asks someone hurrying in the opposite direction.

"No, it is the police."

"Police? What are they doing?"

"They are checking tax receipts," he answers and hurries away.

It is too late for Audu to slip out of sight. One of the officers approaches him and demands, "Where is your tax receipt?"

"It is in my room," he answers with a nervous, stuttering voice.

"You do not have it?"

"It is in my room," he answers too loudly.

"You, stand with them," the policeman says, pointing to a large group gathered on one side of the road.

"Let me go to my room and get my papers," Audu begs.

"No, stand over there."

Many pedestrians and cyclists had been stopped. They were asked to produce evidence that they had paid their taxes.

"You who do not have your receipts will now go with us," one of the policemen orders. Walking close together, they sometimes bump into each other. The group follows the officers to the charge office. Those with cycles push them along the way. Another police officer follows those who have been arrested.

◆ ◆ ◆ ◆ ◆

As they are taken away, another scene occurs in the market. Yahaya, son of the juju priest from Barikin Biyu, enters. He stops in front of a booth selling shoes and sandals. He furtively looks to be sure that his route of escape is clear. It's an early hour. Only a few shoppers are in this part of the market. Yahaya picks up a pair of sandals that look to be his size. He tucks them under his arm and runs.

"Thief! Thief!" the shopkeeper shouts angrily. He chases after Yahaya. Others join in the pursuit.

The cry, "Thief! Thief! Stop that thief!" is shouted above the other market noises.

Yahaya drops the sandals but doesn't slow down. Perspiration covers his body. The sound of his pursuers' feet hitting the ground rings in his ears. They are getting closer to him. Soon, a rough hand touches him. Another grabs his shirt and tears it, causing him to stumble. The next hand knocks him to the ground. He can taste the blood from his cut lips.

"Thief! Thief!" the mob shouts, as they all try to get their hands on him. The anger of those nearest him is dissipated by their blows. Yahaya lies bruised and bleeding on the dirty ground of the market. Two police officers come and take him away. Some of the crowd that had chased him follow. They leave the market.

Reaching the charge office, one officer writes out a statement explaining the crime. He reads it to Yahaya. He asks him to sign it on the line he is pointing out to him.

"I cannot write."

"Then place your thumb print on it," an officer instructs. An ink pad is shoved across the desk toward him. Yahaya does as he is told. But does so with an air of arrogance. Such insolence had not been evident during the cries of "thief" that had followed him until his capture.

"Come," demands one of the police.

Slowly, Yahaya rises and follows him. He is led into a cell used to hold men when they are first brought to the police station. Several others are already in the room. Two sit on the floor with their backs to the wall. They say little. But one man laughs when each new person is brought in. Yahaya isn't there long before the police bring in some others to be locked up. He watches as the door opens and four men enter. Immediately, he recognizes Audu.

"Audu, Audu, what are you doing here?" Yahaya asks, as he moves toward the only one he knows.

Audu doesn't like Yahaya because he is a troublemaker. Yet Audu speaks to him and smiles. "I did not have my tax receipt with me so they brought me here. If they will let me go to my room, I can get it. It is in my box there. Why are you here?"

"I was looking at a pair of sandals and the useless trader started shouting, 'Thief! Thief!' I was frightened and ran. That is why I am here. As soon as they understand, they will let me go."

Pausing for only a few seconds Yahaya continues, "Have you found Laraba and the evil ones?" Without waiting for an answer, he continues. "I just came from home. Everyone is anxious to know if the twins have been destroyed. Because of them, trouble has come to me and to our village. The rains stopped too soon. The crops are turning brown. If you had only done what you should have done that night, then we would not have all this trouble! You and I would not be in this jail."

Audu and Yahaya speak in their heart language. Audu is glad the others don't understand their conversation. Although Yahaya's words make Audu angry, he tries not to show it.

"No. I have not found them. Do you know where they are?

"No, I do not know where they are."

"Then why do you talk so much?"

"I have been in Danbar for only one day. I will find them!"

"You talk like a foolish man."

"Say what you will. I will find them and do what should have been done!"

"Yahaya, come," commands a police officer.

"You will see. They will let me go." Yahaya turns and looks at Audu with contempt. "Now I will do what you were not able to do."

Audu is frightened by Yahaya's talk. He feels Yahaya can find people from their village living here. He might be able to do what Audu couldn't do. Or, they might be just empty words. This heightens his urgency in finding Laraba. He looks around at the others taken with him and asks, "When will they call us?"

"Who knows?" one of them answers.

"My receipt is in my room. If they will only let me go, I can produce it."

"If you have paid, why did you fail to have it with you?"

"Those who check in my village know that I pay my taxes. They do not question me. I brought the receipt with me to the city. But I fail to carry it on me. Without difficulty, I can get it. If they will only let me go to my room."

"They will not let you go."

"What, then, will happen?"

"Who knows?"

With a deep frown on his face, Audu paces up and down in the cell. He hardly hears a fellow prisoners say, "You will have to wait and see."

The door opens, and an officer says, "Do any of you want to pay your taxes now?"

Although still ill at ease, Audu's attention is sharply brought back to his cell. Here's a chance to get out of jail. So he says, "I would like to speak to the collector."

"That is not the answer to my question. I asked, 'Do you want to pay?'"

"I have paid and I have a receipt."

"Let me see it."

"It is not here, but in my room. Let me go for it. I will return quickly."

"You cannot go until your taxes are paid."

"Then I will pay again." None of the other prisoners says anything.

"Come," the policeman commands Audu.

He leaves the cell and follows the man down the hall to another room. Sitting at a desk is a man in a uniform. It's different from those worn by the police. He smiles and speaks to Audu.

"You want to pay?"

"I have paid, and my paper is with me here in the city. It is in my box in my room."

"You cannot go until you pay."

Audu has an idea. "Let me leave the amount for the taxes with you. When I return with my receipt, you can return my money."

After handing the man the money, Audu stretches out his hand for confirmation. The man scribbles a note on a scrap of paper and hands it to him.

Going out the door, Audu asks a man leaning against the wall out-side for directions to the street where he is staying. Although it takes him about ten minutes, he goes directly to his room. With his small key, he unlocks his box, lifting out everything as he searches for his receipt. Finding it, he immediately hides his remaining money under the straw mattress. He leaves his clothes scattered on the floor and on his bed.

In haste, he returns to the police station. He almost runs into a woman. She's carrying a huge load of firewood on her shoulders. When she sees him swiftly approaching her, she moves to the side of the road, trying to avoid him. Nevertheless, a piece of wood falls from the cone-shaped carrier. She stops. With her right foot, she pulls the wood to her left leg and manages to bring it up high enough for her to reach it. Her left hand steadies the container. With her right hand, she places the piece of wood back in her carrier, then hurries on down the road.

Audu apologizes to her. She doesn't seem to understand him. He stands a few moments wondering how she had gotten the heavy load to her shoulders. It must have taken at least two men to lift that amount of wood up. She probably lives several miles out of town, he thinks. Remembering the task at hand, he turns and hurries away.

Arriving at the police station, Audu goes straight to the room where he talked with the tax collector. He raps on the door. There is no answer. He pounds on it. After the third time of knocking, a policeman strolls down the hall to see what he wants.

"Who are you looking for?"

"The tax collector."

"He is not here today."

"But I talked to him just a few minutes ago in this very room."

"You must be mistaken."

"No, I am not mistaken."

The man opens the door. There's no one behind the desk. The room is completely empty.

"Perhaps it was another room," Audu says.

"That one?" the policeman asks, pointing to the room where Audu and the others had been kept.

"No, that is not the room. That is where I was first put."

"Which room then?"

"I do not know. I do know that, just a little while ago, I gave a man in uniform some money. He was to hold it until I returned with my tax receipt. Here is my paper." Audu holds it out for the man to see.

"Well there is no one here now."

"Then where did he go?"

"I have shown you there is no one here."

"What am I to do?"

"There is nothing to do."

"But I need my money back."

"There is no one here to help you. You are mistaken. Leave or I will arrest you."

◆ ◆ ◆ ◆ ◆

Without further word, Audu turns and walks out of the jail. With stooped shoulders and dragging feet, he starts toward the market. He thinks about all that has happened—the words of Yahaya—the loss of his money. His mind is filled with questions. *What's going on? Where is Yahaya? Is he even now looking for Laraba and the twins?* He's sure his people in this city will help him. He considers trying to locate Yahaya. He hates that man and would like to destroy him. *How many other things are going to happen to me? Is all of this the results of the two not being destroyed? Are the gods punishing me for that?*

Seeing a tall tree near the road, Audu goes over to sit on the ground beside it. Leaning his back against the trunk, he wipes his frowning face with sweaty palms. After puzzling over his situation for a while, he closes his eyes to rest them. There's no answer before him. His money is dwindling. There's no one to help him. He continues to dwell on all of the bad things that are happening. He begins to think about going home. Maybe Laraba has returned.

Laboring to raise himself up, he feels the rumbling in his stomach and remembers he hasn't eaten today. He wants to find food. After that, he'll return to his room. He needs to decide what to do. Slowly, he lifts his heavy feet. He trudges along the dirt path. With his face toward the ground, he doesn't notice anyone or anything. Among the people he meets along the way is Victoria. He doesn't know her. He almost stumbles into her. She stares at Audu, recognizing he is from a tribe not far from her home. She feels sorry for him, as he seems so lonely and distressed. She almost speaks to him but instead she moves on to meet Laraba a few blocks away.

◆　◆　◆　◆　◆

After being caught and charged, Yahaya is led to the courthouse across the street. Entering a large room filled with many people, the officer looks for a seat. Since only the back row of benches is empty, he motions for Yahaya to sit there and plops down beside him.

After waiting several hours, Yahaya hears his name called. He jumps up. The guard stands and directs him to follow. Moving down the aisle Yahaya makes sneaky glances at those on either side. No one responds to his stares. His questioning eyes reveal his fear.

Stopping before the tall desk in front of them, Yahaya trembles at the sight of the man dressed in a long black robe and wearing a white wig. He has never seen anyone dressed like that in his own village.

To himself he mumbles, "Why am I here? Because I did not run fast enough? Was it the quick cry of the shopkeeper? Those who joined in the chase? Were those the reasons? No, it is because of the twins—they are the cause of my capture."

He quickly turns his head when again he hears, "Yahaya!"

"Sir?"

Another person from the right at a small wooden desk is speaking. "Listen to this." He reads the statement to which Yahaya had put his print.

"Is it true?"

He looks down, but doesn't answer. Perspiration beads upon his forehead.

"Answer! Is it true?"

Rubbing his hands down the sides of his garment to dry them, he shuffles his feet. He continues to look at the floor.

The man behind the big desk says, "Answer the questions. Is the statement you gave true?"

Yahaya's doesn't lift his eyes, nor does he speak.

"Answer the questions now!" demands the man in the strange dress.

"The devil made me do it. The devil made me do it," he blurts out.

"I find you guilty and sentence you to three months."

The policeman reaches out and takes him by the arm. "Come," he says, though not unkindly.

As they leave the room, Yahaya whispers, "Who is that man sitting up so high?"

"He is the judge," explains the officer. "It is his responsibility to decide what to do with people who break the law."

Without another word, Yahaya is taken from the court room. They walk to a building down the road. There his guard opens the double doors. Then he places his left hand on Yahaya's shoulders and nudges him in. Pausing before a door with a small window, the officer knocks on it with the long, round stick he's been carrying in his right hand. First, the window opens. A pair of eyes look out. Then the door swings in. Yahaya is directed to enter. The passageway is locked behind them.

"Go to that room," a different man commands, pointing to the end of the hall.

"You may go now, Corporal."

The new watchman goes with Yahaya to the bathroom. There he is instructed to take off his clothes and take a bath. Pointing to an opening in the wall, the man says, "There is the shower. After you bathe, put on these clothes. Place your own clothes and stuff in this small wooden box. I will be waiting for you here."

Yahaya goes in the room and begins slowly to undress. Taking his time to carefully wash the blood from his cuts and bruises, he finishes his bath and steps out of the shower. He dresses in the prison garments and lays his things in the box that was given to him. Returning to the outer room, he discovers the uniformed man is sitting in a chair, waiting to take Yahaya somewhere else.

"Bring your box and come with me."

Yahaya doesn't say anything, but follows as he is told. Moving down a hall, they come to a door upon which is stenciled, "Store Room."

The guard unlocks the door and instructs him, "Put your box there." He points to an empty space on a shelf.

After Yahaya lifts it into place, the officer takes a key from the ones he holds in his hands and locks the door behind them. They proceed further down the same corridor. Their next stop is a cell.

"This is your room," the man tells Yahaya, as he unlocks the door for him to enter. When Yahaya is securely inside, he bolts it back.

There is no one else here. And no one is in any of the other cells. The only sound is the echo of the guard walking away. There are four places to sleep. After surveying the space, Yahaya goes to the barred window. It's high. But by standing on his tiptoes and drawing himself up, he can see outside. The yard is desolate! The ground is barren, without even one tree. Narrow streaks on the ground show that it has recently been swept with a straw broom.

Tired and sore, Yahaya turns. He sits on one of the hard beds. In a few moments, he stretches out with his hands under his head. Staring at the ceiling, he mumbles to himself, "This has all happened so quickly. It is because of Laraba and the two. If she had not given birth to them, this would not have happened to me."

Anger creases his face, as he mutters to himself. "They must be destroyed. I will find them. I will do it. Today, tomorrow, as soon as I can, I will do it. What that weak one could not do, I will do. As soon as I get out of this place, I will go to the section of the town where my people live. They will be glad to help me find those sources of evil and destroy them. There is a river out from this town. I will take them there and throw them in. They will drown and that will end my trouble."

His face relaxes. Relieved now that he has a plan of action, he closes his eyes and drifts off to sleep. After a nap, Yahaya opens his eyes and stares around with a puzzled expression. He runs his hands over the coarse, rough bed covering. Looking up, he sees one bulb, enclosed in a wire basket, hugging the ceiling. He swings his legs out of the bed and sits up. Stomping his feet, he returns to the window. Again, he stretches to look outside the small, barred window. The shadows have become long. As he stands there, he shakes his fist and vows, "I will destroy them!"

Somewhere a door opens. The sound of many feet rings through the building as they walk toward Yahaya. The cell door is unfastened and opened. Three, garbed in the same kind of clothes as him, enter.

"Welcome to our cell. We are pleased to have you join us," says one of the men, as he enters.

"Thank you, but I cannot say it is good to be here."

They laugh, "You will find it a good place."

"Where have you come from?"

"Work."

"You mean they allow you to work?"

"You must know it is not a case of being permitted to work. We are forced to work."

"What do they make you do?"

"Most of us have to cut grass and clean the yards of the government houses."

"I will not do it!"

"We all have to work. You will, too. How long are you to be here?"

"The judge said three months, but I will not stay here that long."

"You talk foolishly."

"You just wait and see," he snaps.

"This is not a bad place. The food is free. Our clothes are provided. The work is not hard," comments one who had not spoken before.

"And they do not charge for the room," laughs another, as he sits on one of the other beds.

"I am going to leave. I have something important to do."

"How will you get out?"

"I do not know yet, but you will see."

"You talk a lot," another man contends. "What else can you do? No, do not tell me. I do not want to know."

Noting Yahaya's glaring eyes, two of the prisoners see he is angry. Not wanting trouble in their cell, they jump down from the top bunks where they had been sitting. One says, "It's time for food. Soon we will be called."

Yahaya remains seated on his bunk. "I do not want food in this place. I'm sure it is not worth eating."

"It is good food. If you do not eat now, you will get nothing else to eat tonight."

Hearing the guards walking in their direction, the three men turn to look at them. They know they will soon be able to eat. They are hungry. A key turns in the lock of their cell. As the door opens, Yahaya's three cellmates start to leave.

One of them turns to him and says, "Come on. Perhaps you will see someone you know. Anyway, they will not let you stay here alone. If you try not to go, you are just asking for trouble."

Without answering, Yahaya joins them. He goes with the others to the wing of the jail where the dining hall is located. He lifts his eyebrows when he sees so many men. There must be 70 prisoners and many guards. At first, the noise of clanging plates, many men talking and benches being moved is deafening. Soon, it becomes quiet with only the sounds of eating.

Yahaya's cell mates whisper to each other. "He must have forgotten his comment about the food not being fit to eat."

"Yes. Look at him! He devours it like he thinks he will never eat again."

After the meal, the men are allowed to go to the yard for exercise. Yahaya studies the faces around him. Turning to another prisoner who is about his age, Yahaya asks, "Why are so many of these men so young?"

"Most of them are here with a sentence for petty crimes. Obviously thievery is appealing to them as the way to get things they cannot hope to afford," the man explains.

"Evidently they gave little thought to the consequences of being caught."

"And why are you here?"

"It was a misunderstanding, and I was charged."

"That has happened to many of us," laughs the man.

No longer interested in this conversation, Yahaya ambles across the yard. There are many different languages. Few he recognizes. He walks up to an older man who looks familiar and greets him. The man is from a village near Yayaha's home and understands him. They begin to talk.

"It surprises me that among so many there are no arguments or boisterous conversations."

"That would only cause trouble."

"Has something weakened and placated them all?"

Although the man doesn't answer, Yahaya continues, "I do not want the same thing to happen to me. Besides, I have a task to perform. I will find a way to get out of this place soon,"

◆　◆　◆　◆　◆

Returning to the market, Audu first goes to the cloth seller's stall. It remains closed. With bent shoulders, he shuffles along. Dejection fills his mind and heart. Although it is only eleven o'clock, the sun is hot. The day is discouraging. His experience with the police has stunned him. Those men had literally robbed him. They took his money under false pretense. They are no better than Yahaya. His money is going fast, especially with this last misfortune, and there's little prospect of getting any more. His nerves are raw and taut. His time in the city is growing short. There's not enough money to stay much longer. Then he thinks he mustn't get too discouraged or stop looking. There are still places he hasn't traveled.

Audu goes to the side of the market that he hadn't been before. There he comes to an area where musical instruments are made and sold. On one side a man is carving four holes about two inches apart on a large hollow reed. Colorful red and blue plastic string is wrapped around each end of the nineteen-inch long stalk. Audu knows that a man will blow in the end. His fingers will rhythmically cover the large holes. The musical sounds will be interesting. There are piles of long bamboo leaves folded in triangular shapes encasing seed. These are attached to each other with strong string to be wrapped around the legs. They rattle as one dances around.

There are also different kinds of drums. Then he sees one of his favorite instruments. Made of bamboo shoots, it has a six-inch wide and about fifteen-inch-long flat base. Attached to this are fifteen strings in sets of three. Each string is wrapped with different amounts and lengths of thin bamboo strips in the center and at each end. Small seeds are enclosed in an area behind the strings. He notices some that are twice as wide as the one he saw at first. He can visualize a young man walking down the road, holding the instrument in front at his waist, strumming the strings with his thumbs. Their woeful sounds would suit his mood right now. For several minutes, Audu is engrossed in watching the men at work. Suddenly, he brings himself back to his reasons for being here and walks away.

On one street, in every third stall, one can purchase radios or phonographs. The sellers compete for attention by playing their records at full volume. A person can't hear one for the others. This is more disturbing than many drummers playing different tunes all at one time. Audu admits to himself that those who work near them or those who pass by must not even hear them.

Down another street, he sees people selling grain, onions, peppers, tomatoes, and a variety of other foods. Four large lorries are being unloaded at the same time. A man on one lorry helps each carrier place a big bag on his head so he can easily carry it.

Audu proceeds through the market. The atmosphere of the city is difficult for him to understand. Everyone is in a hurry. It reminds him of a young, strong dog in chase after a big rat in a clear field, or of a hawk plunging down to catch a chicken, or of an antelope frightened from a water hole during the dry season. Even when people stop to talk or answer a question, they seem hurried. They become fidgety and anxious. Their voices are rushed and tight. Their eyes swiftly look here and there. It's as if, even though someone is here in this place, his mind is elsewhere.

Audu realizes it will take him a long time to cover the central market—it can't be done in two days or even three. *How many stalls are there? Everything costs so much! It's too dear here. This isn't a good place to live.* The oppressiveness of the city smothers him. The closeness is greater than the heaviest harmattan. It's stifling! He feels like the strongest wrestler has cut off his breath, and he's struggling to breathe.

Audu's forehead creases with a frown, as he mutters to himself, "There is no air, no life, no joy in this big city."

He shrugs his shoulders and remembers he didn't come to the city to live. It doesn't matter whether he likes it or not. He's here to find Laraba. She may not be in this vast market, but maybe he will meet someone who can help him find her. The day is young and the market is large.

Drumming begins deeper in the market, so he walks in that direction. The butchers arrive with freshly-killed beef, and the drummers announce the meat is ready for sale. Who could believe the many vultures flying above? They land atop different stalls, waiting to swoop down and grab a piece of meat that falls to the ground. With open mouth, he stares incredulously at the vultures. Audu moves to stand at the end of the row of tables where the butchers cut and sell the meat. From this vantage point, he can see almost everyone who comes to buy. Eagerly, he watches. Soon all the meat is sold and the crowd moves away. He shakes his head again with regret, realizing he hasn't seen anyone he recognizes.

As he reaches one of the major roads that border the market, he notices many running back from the road. Between two stalls, he sees a large army lorry. Audu watches soldiers with rifles climb down from their truck. They advance with an arrogance he fears. After searching one corner of the market, they return. Apparently, they didn't find anything.

On the other side of the road, he sees a group of men sitting on the ground. As he draws near them, he discovers some young men gambling in the shade of a chinaberry tree. They are playing Ayo. Taking turns, each man picks up a handful of nuts from the larger hole at his end of the board game. With speed, nuts are dropped in one hole after another around the 12 holes until it is the next person's turn. Gambling didn't bring them from their villages to the town, but this is the only thing they have found. Success and money have cleverly eluded them. The prosperous life, a joke now, hasn't become a reality. Audu doesn't speak. He watches. Realizing that he doesn't know any of the men, he soon leaves.

A small, dirty, ragged boy lifts the nub of his right arm for Audu to see. The tragic accident had brought the boy a thing of value, a beggar's dream. Audu reaches into his pocket, finds a penny, and gives it to the boy. The boy responds with a smile.

CHAPTER SIXTEEN

Unfortunate Contact

While comparing the differences in this market to the one at home, Audu notices a man standing nearby. He decides to speak to him. "Greetings. How are you?"

The stranger looks questionably at Audu. He returns a hesitant response, "I am well. How is your day?"

"I am trying to find someone, but without success. Are you from Danbar?"

"No. but I have brothers who live here. What about you?"

Uncertain about this man, Audu doesn't share his real purpose for being here, but says, "I am looking for some of my people."

"Did you come here without the names and locations of any of your people?" asks the man.

"I am afraid so. Perhaps you know a way to locate someone?"

"No, I am sorry I do not know. I wish you good luck. Now I must go," states the stranger, as he walks farther into the market.

Audu stands, looking at the ground. He rubs his face. He wonders why the man wasn't willing to assist. Besides, why hadn't he realized it would take a long time to look for Laraba and the two. He should have brought more money. He needs to count how much is left. He returns to the food seller's table and sits on a bench facing the market. Audu hardly notices the short, thin, well-dressed man who is walking toward him. The man suddenly sits down beside him.

In a soft voice, he calmly says, "It is disheartening when you cannot find a lost one, isn't it?"

Audu stares at the man in surprise. He's never seen this man before. "How do you know I am looking for someone?"

"Several times I have seen you wandering the market, intently gazing at everyone you pass. It is sad when one cannot find the one he is seeking. And the shortage of money adds to your troubles."

Again Audu questions how the man could know that he is even now worrying about money. What magical powers does this man possess?

"Alas, it is so," he agrees with the sympathetic fellow.

"Perhaps I can help you," the stranger suggests. "Finding a lost one is very difficult. But perhaps I can help you with your money problem. I have a friend who has a unique ability. He can double money. Often he has helped me and others, so I know he will help you."

"What do you mean?"

"If you give him ten pounds, he can return your ten pounds and give you ten more, or whatever amount you give him," he states in a subdued voice.

"You lie. No one can do that!"

The man's eyes cloud and he looks away. With a quivering voice, he replies, "I am only trying to help you. You do not have to be offended."

Audu is sorry that he has spoken so unkindly. "It is true that I have used most of my money. I have only a little left."

"My friend will double that for you. I know he will because you are my friend. If you will give me what you have, I will go to him and return with double the amount."

Still doubting, but obviously impressed and considering the possibility, Audu asks, "Will he do this for me?"

"How fortunate you are! Today is the very day this can be done. Yes, he will do it for you because you are my friend."

This new acquaintance has kind words. He shows an apparent sincere concern. There is an air of assurance. These impress Audu. But he feels some apprehension. "How can I be sure he can do this today?"

Detecting Audu's interest in getting more money, the man takes several crisp new notes from his suit pocket and shows them to Audu. "Look, I gave him four notes early this morning, and in a matter of minutes he returned eight notes. See! Count them for yourself."

Audu counts the eight notes and looks again at the man, wondering what to do.

"Trust me, I can help you in your time of great need."

"Let me follow you to your friend's and observe his actions to learn how this is done."

"I would, but he will only allow his special friends to enter his place. Sorry. But I will assure you he can double your money today because he has done the same for me this very day," the man states in his calm and confident manner.

Audu considers the man once more. He feels grateful for his concern and respect. So he carefully takes from his pocket several pound notes. As he begins to count them, he remembers those he has hidden under his mattress in his room. In his hand are five notes, rumpled and dirty. He hands the man three of the notes. "Take these and have him double them for me."

"Give me the other two, also. He can increase five as easily as three."

"No, for him to increase three will be a kind and generous thing."

The man senses that it would be unwise to argue. "You wait here. I will return shortly."

Soon the man is out of Audu's sight, as he hurries away into the crowd. Time passes. The stranger doesn't return. Growing anxious, Audu walks back and forth in front of the food seller's table. He begins wringing his hands. He starts going toward the market to look for the man, but decides he needs to stay where the man can find him, as he would never be able to find him in the crowd. Perhaps he couldn't find his friend, or that man wouldn't agree to help him. Maybe he got lost. So Audu sits back down on the bench by the food seller's counter.

After a long wait, he mutters to himself, "Why, oh, why does he not return?"

Dejected and weary, he stumbles off. He feel like the weight of the world is on his shoulders. He goes only a short distance, but stays near enough to see the food seller's stall. He stands on the side of the road and looks across at the big, spreading mango tree, standing tall and strong. It has an abundance of lush, green foliage. The fruit is slightly yellow and will soon be ready to pick.

He notices the tailor who sits under it on a small wooden folding chair. He peddles the treadle of his Singer sewing machine. It's a different kind of machine from the ones he saw earlier that ran by someone turning the wheel with his hand. This time, the man is mending the seat of a pair of trousers, the most common place for a patch. He has set up his shop in the cool shade, in sight of those who might want garments made or mended. In a small box at his side are his scissors, thread, needles, and other items needed in his profession.

Again he looks toward the market, wondering when the stranger will return. Audu had heard about people who could double your money, but now he begins to question the wisdom of giving the man some money.

In front of the tree is a well-used, gray metal box containing the tools of a bicycle repairman. Five or six cycles are parked in the shade beside the tree, waiting their turn to be fixed. The worker is busy with a hand pump as he puts air into a recently patched rubber tire. He draws the handle up and stoops slightly as he thrusts it down. At the top of each pump, he shoves it half-way down, then quickly lifts it again before forcing it all the way down. This seems to cause the air to enter the tire more quickly.

Out of the corner of his eyes, he sees a man in a suit and starts toward him. He shouts to him. Before Audu can reach him, the man is gone. Then he realizes that that man is much taller than the one to whom he had given his money.

On the other side of the tree is a large, cracked, clay water container. It has a tin lid covering it to keep out insects and the droppings from the tree. It's time for the Muslims' evening prayers. Men and boys come to get water in tin cans to prepare themselves for prayer. Each takes the water and sits on a nearby cement wall or squats down. Carefully, each washes his hands, forearms, face, and feet, then rinses his mouth. One wears socks, which he removes to wash his feet. He puts his socks on again but not his shoes. Though the people's shoes are removed, their caps remain on their heads. After these preparations, each one is ready to pray. They enter the reserved area of ground near the tree. Although there is no building, an entrance with a line of stones points them toward the East.

This group doesn't pray in unison, unlike those who rise, kneel, put their faces to the ground and sit up, moving as one. Rather they pray, each as he comes. After the ritual of bowing and rising, the hands bring forth prayer beads, which are fingered one by one.

Each bead represents a prayer. Audu watches them and wonders about their behavior. How strange are their movements. He knows very little of their religion, since he has not seen any of its followers back home.

Again, Audu strains to see if there is a man anywhere wearing a suit. He reaches into his pocket to be sure his two pounds remain. As he looks to the left, he notices a man sitting beside a pole for the electric wire. He sells sundry items. The trader spends much time arranging his goods in attractive piles and seeing that all is in order. His "shop" contains cigarettes, which can be purchased as a single stick or in a package. There are also small boxes of "Three Crown Matches" made in Nigeria. Narrow strips of rubber hold the stacks of cigarettes in place, yet a single pack could be removed easily without disturbing the others. On the same tray, but in front of the packages, are kola nuts and two kinds of sweets. Audu watches as a man and woman come to the trader. They buy several pieces of cellophane wrapped candy from a large bag. After opening the bag, the trader places the remaining pieces in the display tray. Soon, a man comes up and buys two cigarettes, which the trader takes from a tin and carefully hands to the customer. One is immediately placed between his lips. The other is tucked into his shirt pocket for another time.

Business seems to be good on this street, far from the busy market, but near many homes. These traders are not the only ones there. Sitting several yards away is another man with a suitcase opened to show his wares. Two men sit nearby, talking softly. Many children pass by, but few buy. A group of boys enthusiastically play soccer in an open space nearby.

Behind this is an attractive, neatly-painted, two-story house. Evidently it is the home of one who is well-to-do. Audu sees three neatly dressed youth at the house. One man lucky enough to possess a small car comes driving up the road to join them. Another young man is standing on the veranda upstairs, combing his hair with a wide-toothed comb. He looks into a small mirror. Apparently, he is pleased with what he sees because he smiles. He turns and calls down to his friends.

As it grows later, the sun is fast running away. Audu begins to be hungry, so he goes back to sit on the food seller bench. She is packing up her things to go home. It is too late to get a meal. He sighs.

"Why doesn't he return?" he whispers. "Why did I give my money to a stranger? Come back, come back," is his mumbled plea as he anxiously stares into the faces in the distance.

Audu looks around but finds no source of strength for himself and his situation. His eyes grow glassy, as he thinks how strange it is that no matter what your difficulties are, the world seems to go on with little concern for you. For others, there appears to be meaning. For himself, Audu questions it. Others don't know his trouble. If they do, they don't care. Wearily, he lifts himself to his feet and looks about once more. Many people are leaving the market. It is growing dark. Audu feels like weeping. His clothes are damp from the heat. *What a fool I have been!*

He strains once more, searching the crowd for the face of the stranger, then stumbles off into the dark toward his room. Again, he's discouraged and defeated. It has been another day of great weariness. Forgetting about his hunger, he doesn't bother to purchase food. It seems impossible that he could move through a town and have so many things happen to him. Yahaya is the only familiar person he's seen, but he only brought trouble. He shakes his head that not one thing has happened to help him find Laraba.

He goes into the entrance hall that leads to his small, dull, dingy room. This place has come to stand for failure. Now he doesn't care what happens to himself.

CHAPTER SEVENTEEN

A Wise Woman

In one corner of the dimly lit hallway is a pile of maize husks. Hanging from a peg driven into the mud wall is an old burlap bag. Many patches bear witness to its long and valued career. Cobwebs covered with dust run their course back and forth from the bag to the rafters of the roof. The bag has been long forgotten. An old hoe, a cutlass, a digger, a pick and an extra handle, implements for the farm, lay nearby. Now these are coated with mud and rust, telling of their present uselessness. There beside the once useful goods sits the old woman on a faded and dirty mat. Audu doesn't want to talk.

However, with concern, she speaks, "You have returned?"

At first, Audu doesn't answer. But then he says, "I have returned. It has been a fruitless day." He takes in a long breath and slowly lets it out. "It is not possible to find someone in this city. There are too many here. If Laraba is here, she has just vanished." He stoops down and sits on his haunches. The deepening lines on his face show his despair.

Taiwo brings a lamp to give light to the hallway. After greeting Audu, he leaves to eat his meal of porridge made from dried corn.

It is cool here. Soon, the sweat dries on Audu's face and neck. He looks into the sunken eyes of the woman. Her eyes that have long been blind have left only grotesque holes outlined above by a few white hairs. Her aged face, scarred by tribal marks, is as mellow as an overripe mango.

With toothless mouth, she tries to encourage him. She says, "You will find her. She will come to you." She pauses, as a bleating goat, closely followed by two boys, runs through the hall. She smiles. "The boys have no trouble. Their only desire is to chase the goat. For them that is life."

"That is not life. They do not know."

"No, this is life for them and it is meaningful. Life has great meaning for all. But, it is not always the same for everyone."

"You don't know life, old woman."

"Yes," in patience she answers, "perhaps you are right. But I know some things." Then she adds, "I have felt the dryness and smelled the rain.

I have heard the crowing of the cock, the beginning of a new day.
I have heard the cluck of the hen, the beginning of a new life.
I have heard the winging of the bat, the beginning of a new night.
I have heard the snap of the trap, the ending of life.
You will find her. I know you will meet success."

Audu's mind races to his home and village. He sees the cluster of huts on the hillside. His mind takes him back to his childhood. He decides to talk to the old woman about his family. He tells her his older brother is Bala, who used to sit on a large rock watching the flock of ragged sheep and goats. Their coats were matted and dirty from the last rains and the thorny shrubs on the hillside. The care of the animals brought him satisfaction and enjoyment. They responded to his care. Their offspring grew quickly and brought a good price in the market. Bala loved the farm. But there is one thing he loved more than the farm and animals—his books.

He shares about the day his brother left the village to go to a high school in another part of their country. He hadn't been home for several years. Next year or the year after he's to return. Often they had talked about the school. Audu once told him, "You have your books. You can return and spend your time in the valley. You'll miss the excitement of life." He told the women that it had not been spoken unkindly, because he was proud of his brother and the things he wanted to do. He, the firstborn, is like their father, kind and gentle.

Audu also tells about Bako, his father. He was a tall man with strong hands and bright eyes. He saw everything. His hair and beard were graying. The beard was growing around the many tribal marks on his face. He was a wise and good man. He wore a smile revealing crooked, yellowed teeth. Often he had led the men of the village in their hunts because he could walk faster and more quietly than the others. His arrows provided fresh meat for his family. His crops were the finest. The walls of his huts were the straightest and strongest. His roofs were the closest woven so no water could enter, even during the heaviest rains and strongest winds.

His wise old friend eagerly listens as he speaks of Uwa, his caring mother. He admits it is the first time in many days he had given any thought to her. There she stands pulverizing corn. *I can almost hear the sound of the pounding stick striking the grain in the large wooden mortar.* She often wears a blue and black cloth, one she had woven from cotton thread dyed in their vat. The cloth neatly drawn together under her arms gives freedom for her task. It has only one opening, the one down the left side. She wears it neatly, as neatly as she does everything. A thin, pale-orange cloth band about her forehead completes her attire.

Uwa is a kind, patient woman, a source of strength for her family. She is the first to rise in the morning, having the food prepared before the others turn on their mats to look out at the new day. Many come to their compound to buy the mats she weaves. Her designs are interesting, her colors long-lasting. As a small boy, he had watched her at work. She selected first the green, then the tan, red, and blue, and finally the brown-colored straw. She discarded those which were not strong or bright.

He feels again the touch of his mother's hands the day he had fallen from the rocks and cut his leg. She had tenderly washed it and applied the medicine that would bring healing. She had brought him cool water and the best fruit. There in the comfort of her hut, she had cared for him until his leg had healed.

Quiet for a few moments he imagines a picture of Uwa. It makes him think of the old woman sitting before him. For the first time he decides to be kinder and show her tenderness.

Then Audu continues his conversation about his home and family as he tries to catch a vision of his youth and happiness. He talks of his sister Riti, who often wore a white cloth, usually hung simply around her waist. It was like that worn by most maidens of his village. Her copper earrings hung low, glittering in the sun. She was a good cook. She kept their hut and the compound around it swept clean. She didn't leave the water low in the water pot for very long. The stream was close by, so she saw no reason for not having the container full at all times. Riti liked fun too. Singing, dancing, and drumming brought a smile to her face. She liked to laugh and to have those around her joyful and full of amusement. A year before Laraba came, Riti had left to go to her husband's home. Audu thinks of her now, though, as if it were yesterday, when they were children running and shouting at each other. Now it seems so long ago.

Audu gets up to leave, but turns to the old woman and says, "Thank you for your encouragement. You are a wise woman. Now I must go."

He goes toward his room. As he enters, his canary greets him with song. It reminds him of happier days gone by.

Other strangers in the city have also brought their birds with them. These beautiful winged creatures seem to help maintain contact with the past and home. Audu's songbird is a comfort. It supports him in this strange and difficult place. Sometimes, when the men return to their rooms, they take their birds and go out on the street to challenge each other. The cages are held close together, and the birds sing. Audu's is one of the very best singers. The only pleasure he has known since coming to the city is when his pet is in full throat.

Suddenly, he is interrupted, as his name is called, "Audu, Audu, someone has come asking for you."

This is the first time anyone has looked for him since he rented the room from Taiwo. Audu begins to tremble with excitement. His hopes of finding Laraba rush into his mind. Moving toward the door, he tries to steady his hands and hopes that his voice will not waver. Reaching the door, he opens it smoothly. There he sees a friendly, smiling face. A young man is holding a crudely built cage that houses a beautiful yellow and green bird.

"Audu, I have heard your bird in full throat. He is fine. I have brought mine and want them to sing together. Do you have time to bring yours out?"

"Yes," replies Audu with little enthusiasm. His aroused interest is dashed to bits. Then, noting the man's disappointment, he remembers his responsibility as a host. So Audu adds, "Excuse me. I will get my bird."

Quickly, he returns with his canary. Soon, their two pets join each other in song. Almost immediately, others come to listen. Audu is pleased with the performance of his bird and holds up the painted blue cage in victory.

CHAPTER EIGHTEEN

Yahaya Escapes Jail

In the jail, Yahaya walks away from the man with whom he had been talking. That fellow looks after him with a frown on his face. Entering the large recreation room, Yahaya sees a place where games are played. Books, magazines and a few daily newspapers are provided for those who can read. He goes to a table covered with magazines. Most of the covers are torn off. He selects one with many pictures. He sits in a chair and begins to look at them. Soon he slumps in the seat, fast asleep. A bell ringing awakens him. The magazine has fallen on the floor. He doesn't bother to pick it up but follows the others back to his cell. They say little as they file down the hall. Soon all four of the prisoners in his cell are asleep.

Early the next morning, a bell sounds again, arousing the men. "What does that mean?" Yahaya inquires.

"It is time to prepare for the day. It is our cell's turn to have a shower. Then we will take our food. Afterwards we will go to work."

"Where will we be working?"

"We do not know until the guard tells us."

They shower, eat and go outside. Blinking against the bright sun, the prisoners are divided into groups of five each. Their guard for the day tells the men they will work in the yard of the Senior Police Officer (SPO) today. They move off together. The prisoners are in white uniforms with thin tan stripes; their watchman is dressed in a solid medium-blue uniform. All were made in the prison tailor's shop. A two-foot-long, round, wooden stick is the only weapon the guard carries. It was made in the prison carpenter's shop.

The guard is a large, pleasant man. He only speaks to the prisoners when it's necessary to tell them what to do, showing no concern for them. He does his job with little interest. Yet in his twelve years of service, he hasn't had any difficulties with his prisoners. Yahaya walks near the leader. He doesn't want to call attention to himself by lagging behind. He has a plan. But none of the others know about it. He decides it will not be difficult to find a time and place to get away.

The SPO's house is in the Government Residential Area (GRA). It's a place Yahaya has never been before. Some of the compounds have high fences around them. Seeing some big automobiles in several of the yards they pass, Yahaya says to the other prisoners, "What fine motors they have."

The expatriates who lived here before self-government had planted many flowers and a variety of trees on their lots. Those foreigners, now replaced by Nigerian leaders, had planned for ease and comfort.

Arriving at the SPO's residence, the prisoners are greeted by the yard man.

"Welcome," he says, as he stands from his bent-over position. His cutlass is in his right hand. He had been cutting the grass with this long sharp blade attached to a short, wooden handle. He's relieved at the arrival of help. It's a great task to keep up the huge compound. The grass, the flowerbeds, and the trees all needed tending.

"You are welcome," he speaks again, with a wide grin.

"Thank you," replies the guard, along with one of the prisoners.

"What work do you want the men to do today?"

"We are to weed the flower beds," the gardener answers. Long ago, he learned to include himself in order to get more work out of the prisoners. "Some are to prepare the ground for more flowers. The tools are in the storeroom. Come, I will show you."

Slowly, shuffling their feet, the men follow him. As they begin to work, Yahaya studies the compound. He gives special attention to the roads and paths.

He asks a fellow prisoner, "Where does that road lead?"

The only response is a shrugged shoulder. Yahaya slips away from the group and eyes their watchman. Looking in both directions, he sees no one on the path nor in the nearby compounds. He bends over with his short-handled hoe and begins chopping at the weeds under some nearby trees.

The guard doesn't seem to be paying attention to any of his men. He looks as if he is daydreaming or about to go to sleep on his feet, though nothing is supporting him. The gardener approaches the guard and begins to talk with him. The two laugh about something and continue their conversation. Neither turns around or looks at the workers. Seeing this, the other men also stop working. They begin talking quietly among themselves.

Yahaya strolls off to another flowerbed to the left. He gets closer to the road where they had entered this yard. He works alone, but looks at the guard often.

"Is he really so unaware?" Yahaya mumbles. "Things are going well so far. Which way should I go? But this uniform will tell all who see me that I am a prisoner. I must find other clothes. That should soon be possible," he whispers to himself.

The guard laughs again and turns his back to Yahaya. "Is he is trying to bait me?"

"Does he want me to try to escape? Maybe I have underestimated him. Is there some kind of reward for catching a prisoner who tries to run away? Surely one who does this kind of work cannot be so stupid." he whispers. "I am so alone. That will not stop me. The trouble of the last few days has been caused by the twins. Nothing must be allowed to hamper my responsibility of finding them. Once they are destroyed, good things will be mine again."

The two men keep on talking. The other prisoners are half-heartedly doing their work. Yahaya looks around, but sees no one else in the compound. He slowly slips farther away toward some thick wine-colored bougainvillea bushes between where he and the others are working. The road is only a few feet away. He begins pulling weeds near the bushes. Still, the guard pays no attention. Cautiously and deliberately, he maneuvers to the other side of the bushes. No one even looks in his direction.

He again mumbles to himself, "This is too easy. Maybe I am being set up for a purpose. I did talk a lot about leaving. But what more can they do to me than they are doing now?"

Quietly, dropping his hoe, he reaches the road without arousing suspicion. As he runs along, his eyes dart nervously from side to side. No one is in sight. His breathing becomes steadier.

Quickly, he needs to locate something else to wear. Just then, he looks at a compound on the right side of the road. A washman is hanging up clothes in the back yard. Yahaya stops and slowly moves to the hedgerow where he cannot be seen. As he hides, he mouths,

"Why did I stop so soon? I may be missed already. They will come looking for me. But they are stupid! They will not find me."

The washman finishes hanging up the clothes and goes back to the laundry room. The road is still clear. Yahaya has not been missed yet. He creeps to the corner where the hedge is thicker.

The domestic quarters behind the large main house are between the hedge and the road. He creeps up beside the small structure. Now he has a good view of the road and the drying clothes. He is confident of success.

He hears strained cries from running men. The guard and prisoners speed past him, going too fast to thoroughly seek for the escapee. From the shadows he watches them, unnoticed in his hiding place.

"Will they return and search this place more carefully?" he questions.

A flicker catches his attention. The washman returns with a small pail of clothes to hang on the line. Yahaya watches him carefully. Since his pursuers have all passed by, he doesn't need to be concerned about the road now. The worker takes a faded khaki shirt and a not-so-faded pair of khaki pants out of the pail and hangs them on the line. They are about his size. All he needs to do is wait where he is in this heavy undergrowth until they are dry.

Suddenly, there's a loud cry. Yahaya slips to the ground and draws his legs close to his body. Two cyclists pass by. One of the men calls to the other. They are speaking in a language Yahaya doesn't recognize. He has never been easily frightened before, but now he finds it difficult to control his nervousness. Since the birth of the twins, tension quickly mounts in him.

Sinking back against the building, he mutters, "I must be careful not to let anything cause me to panic. I must do what Laraba or Audu should have done."

Turning his gaze back to the clothes, Yahaya surveys the yard again. It's hot. Almost no moisture is in the air. The things will be dry soon. There are some shrubs near the line. He can hide behind them. It will only take a few moments to get to the clothes. The only movement or activity is from a few birds searching for insects and seeds. Perspiration trickles from under his arms. As he waits, he constantly looks around, fidgeting with sprigs on the ground.

Yahaya takes off his prison shirt. He puts it on again. He looks for a large stick. In a corner by the building, he sees a cutlass. He crawls over and gets it. Perhaps without a shirt on and with the grass cutter in his hand, he would look like a gardener.

Without waiting any longer, Yahaya removes his shirt. He picks up the cutlass and casually but swiftly moves to the clothes line. Deftly he takes the two pieces from the line and quickly returns to his hiding place. Removing his prison trousers, he puts on the slightly damp tan shirt and pants. The trousers are short and the shirt is snug. But they are just what he needs. He never imagined he'd be able to get clothing so quickly. It wasn't difficult. Now if he can only find and destroy the evil ones with as little trouble and as quickly, all will be well again. He takes the prison garb and rolls it into a small bundle. This he tucks under his arm. A tailor in his village can make something out of this cloth. No one will ever know where he got them.

◆ ◆ ◆ ◆ ◆

After her encounter with the people being killed and houses destroyed, Laraba is even more afraid to take the twins away from the house, so they stay at home every day. On the second day of her time in Danbar, Victoria had invited her to join in the trading in a nearby area of the market, but she was afraid of being recognized. She shuddered at the thought of something happening to her babies.

She also remembers that the produce from her farm should be ready to pick. She longs to be at home gathering it and wonders if Audu has thought of harvesting the maize. It becomes harder and harder to stay alone in the compound. Finally one day she decides to go with Victoria. She watches each person who stops to buy. To her surprise no one seems concerned about her twins. In fact, several are interested in seeing them. With relief, she continues to go with Victoria. Then one day a woman comes by. She gasps at the sight of two babies so much alike.

"How can you allow them to live?" she screams in Laraba's mother tongue, as she waves her arms in the air. "Do you not know you are causing evil to mount here!"

Trembling, Laraba grabs the babies up in her arms from the cloth they are lying on beside her. She runs as fast as she can to the house to hide. The woman chases after her.

Victoria catches up with the stranger and grabs her by her shoulders to stop her. The woman is still hollering insults. Victoria struggles to calm her. She tells her, "The babies will not hurt you."

"They will cause much evil if allowed to live any longer. I am surprised you have not already felt their power!" rages the woman, as she turns to face Victoria with fear in her eyes.

After some debate, the woman leaves. Victoria picks up her box of items to sell and returns home. She will need to help Laraba become quiet and settle down. After that, Laraba won't leave their compound for many days.

CHAPTER NINETEEN

Babies In Critical Condition

When Victoria returns home from the market one evening, she finds Laraba sitting on the floor weeping. She places her hand on Laraba's shoulder and asks, "What is the matter?"

"It is the babies. They do not want to eat. They will hardly try to nurse. What am I to do?"

"I have noticed that they cry more lately. Let me help you. Before we begin preparing food, I will take this one for a walk. Maybe it will help to be outside for a while. Then, after we eat, I will walk with the other one."

Laraba nods and leans against the wall, holding her other infant in her arms. As she watches Victoria leave, her sobs grow louder. She wonders what she will do now.

While Victoria walks in the neighborhood, she sees Yahaya down the road talking with a stranger. As she approaches them, she sees his tribal marks. She thinks he looks familiar. She can't remember where she has seen him. So she turns and goes in another direction. She whispers, "Little one, is that someone looking for you?"

When she gets back home, she doesn't tell Laraba about seeing a familiar face. But she says to her, "It might be good for you to stay inside our compound with the infants for a few days. It is too hard for you to carry both of them since they are not feeling well." It's easy for Laraba to agree with Victoria, so she remains in the compound most of the time.

* * * * *

Later, as Laraba dozes, she can vaguely hear the compound noises, but they mean little to her. The babies have been ill for several days. She finds herself sleeping at every opportunity. But sleep doesn't bring rest or peace. Her dreams are many. They are filled with foreboding about her future. She can't live here with Victoria and John forever. *How long have I been here anyway? The days run together and time is of little importance anymore.*

One of the twins whimpers feebly. The other hardly cries at all. Its eyes look weary. They are always hungry, and nursing doesn't seem to satisfy. Their heads are too large for their bodies. Their abdomens are distended. But the rest of their bodies aren't growing. First one and then the other has become listless. Even their weeping has grown weaker. Laraba's hands shake as she cares for them, and tears trickle down her checks when she looks at them.

The children's condition worsens during the night. Crying and trembling, Laraba bangs on Victoria's door, calling to her, "Please, can you help me? The babies are very sick. They will not nurse. Their cries are so weak."

In a sleepy voice, Victoria replies, "I am coming."

For the remainder of the night, neither Laraba nor Victoria sleeps. Their throats feel tight. Pain grips their hearts. They exchange worried looks. Dread hangs in the air surrounding them. Laraba ponders her actions of recent days. This only intensifies her questioning. Since she thinks the gods might hear her, Laraba doesn't share her feelings with Victoria. In her exhausted, debilitated condition, her mind doesn't seem to be her own.

Is this the work of the spirits also? Have I been wrong to oppose the customs of the ancestors by keeping the little ones? If they had been destroyed, this anxiety and torture wouldn't exist. Perhaps the gods will now take them from me. But I haven't given them names, hoping they wouldn't be found by angry gods.

She remembers her joy when one and then the other was able to grasp her finger with its tiny hands. She could wrap her own hand around it and draw it close. Then, she couldn't imagine any evil in them. In her heart, she loves them. This had been growing with each passing day.

Her mind is forced back to the moment's need of caring for the smaller baby. Its dark, glazed-over eyes stare at her face seeking attention. Tears whelm up again. She rocks back and forth with her infant held against her. Her head aches. Her stomach feels tight, as she holds the wee, soft and warm body.

Finally, during the night Victoria suggests, "We need to carry the babies to the General Hospital to get medical help."

Laraba is stunned, "I cannot take them there! I have never been to that place. It is strange and I am afraid to go there."

"They have doctors who know how to help people who are sick, even babies."

"But I have heard about the activities of a hospital. Little of that is encouraging. Strong medicine—the needles—huge machines—crowds of strangers—the odors—many rooms—death and distress." All these things tumble out of her mouth.

"What do you want to do, then?"

"Would not the local juju priest be better?"

"He does not have the power the doctors have." Victoria is careful not to accuse or question Laraba's beliefs too much.

"What about the medicine man?"

"The doctors at the hospital will know more."

"If we go to the juju priest, I would have to confess about the twins. He might do what I could not do. Or Audu either. What about the hospital? Will they not also kill my babies?"

"They will not make you destroy them. I have been there and have received help. Perhaps there would be help for the infants."

Finally, in desperation, and not knowing anything else to do, Laraba agrees, "Should we take them now?"

"We will wait until morning. But we must start early because we do not want to be at the end of the line waiting to see the doctor." Victoria then warns her, "Even then, we will likely have to wait all day."

Before daybreak, Victoria, Laraba, and the two babies begin the long trek to the hospital. A multitude of people is already on the road going to work and to the market. Arriving at the hospital, they get in the long line with the others to fill out some forms and secure a ticket for their turn. Then they take their place in the waiting room. Soon, the crowd is even larger. There aren't enough benches for everyone to have a seat. Some sit on the floor. Others go to sit under a tree in the yard. Being among so many people brings greater dread to Laraba. *What if there should be one in the crowd from home? What will I say? What would I do? Why have I agreed to come here?* Even with Victoria carrying one infant, she knows news of her trouble has traveled before her. Any from her village would know of her action and be greatly vexed with her. She can only imagine what they might do to her now.

Laraba sits close to Victoria. She leans against the wall, attempting to remain unnoticed in the crowd. But being in this new and strange environment, she soon finds herself looking all around, trying to see tribal marks, sizes, and builds of those who surround her. Quietly, she questions Victoria about one thing or another. But she is always careful to speak in their language. She listens to find out if any others are using it. They intently discuss whether any will notice the babies are twins. Maybe not, since they were being carried by two women.

Their attention is taken to a young boy who begins screeching and swinging his arms. Suddenly, his leg thrusts through his long flowing gown. Four men seek to forcibly restrain him. One calls for an object to insert in his mouth. Laraba is surprised at the lad's strength, since he is small. *What will he do if the men are unable to control him?* Soon he is calm. The people again continue their various conversations.

Through an open window, they see a sightless old man sitting on the ground. Numerous flies are attracted by food that he has spilled on his face and down his shirt. His long staff lies beside him. He pays no attention. His attendant is a young boy. The lad leaves the begging bowl. He goes to talk with another child nearby.

About the middle of the morning, a trader begins to pass among the crowd. He seeks to sell bananas, mangoes, oranges, and other food. Laraba and Victoria discuss buying but decide to wait. They hope their number will soon be called. Remembering her card, Laraba looks down. She realizes it is now damp and crumpled. Often she looks up eagerly, hoping they will soon be summoned.

The woman sitting next to them begins applying Vaseline to her baby's bottom. He cries and squirms. Then she digs her fingers into the jar. She rubs some on her own heels. They are cracked and raw from the dry weather. Victoria whispers that she too wishes that she had brought some ointment to soothe her hands, lips, and feet.

As the sun rises higher in the sky, there's a steady stream of those who follow the arrows to the latrine. Others ease themselves at the side of the yard. This never seems to stop. Then they sit to wait their turn to see the doctor. Many sleep now.

It is unusually quiet, when a boisterous vocal explosion is heard at the end of the veranda. A woman begins dickering over the cost of the prescribed medicine. She can't understand why the first price given is also the last one. So she keeps attempting to get the hospital clerk to lower the cost. Stomping off without the medicine, the woman soon realizes she isn't going to be successful getting it for less money—she must pay the full amount. She returns and gives the man her money. Grabbing her child by the arm, she leaves the compound.

"She must be from the bush," speaks an old man sitting nearby. He unwraps a damp cloth from his kola nut. He breaks it. Soon, he passes it to those sitting around him.

"Yes, she certainly is not from our place," responds another, as he bites the bitter nut with orange-stained teeth. Not knowing nor caring that he might spread his illness to those who also share the nut, he hands it to the next person.

A mother tries to pacify her crying little girl. Her large, inflamed legs have a foul odor. She brings out her chewing stick and peels the remaining bark off, then places it in the child's mouth.

An old woman suddenly stands, leans over, and vomits out the window onto the ground near Laraba and Victoria. From the sights, sounds and smells, they know the illnesses are many.

Across from Laraba and Victoria, a woman sits, holding her child on her lap. Flies leisurely crawl around the child's eyes. They go unnoticed by her mother. Only when the child whimpers does the mother pay attention to her.

After several more hours of waiting, Laraba's number is finally called. She, Victoria, and the babies are ushered into a small cubicle. As they enter the room, one of the infants gasps for breath. This brings forth several of those standing around as assistants. One runs for more help.

A gruff, elderly doctor comes at once and begins examining the child. As he does, he constantly mumbles half to himself and half to Laraba and Victoria. "Oh! How sick this baby is! Why have you waited so long to bring this infant to the hospital! It is outrageous that you have waited so long to come. Where do you live?"

"24/5 Pump Street," answers Victoria.

"In this town?"

"Yes, sir."

When he sees there are two, he becomes even more aggravated, "Don't you know these babies are starving to death! That is their illness!"

Frightened by the doctor and the condition of her babies, Laraba looks at the floor. She doesn't say a word. Victoria gently places her hand on Laraba's shoulder and gives her a little squeeze. At the same time, she watches the doctor.

"It will be necessary for the infants to remain in the hospital. I do not expect either to survive. Certainly there is no hope that both can live," the doctor says, without looking in their direction.

Now both Laraba and Victoria can only lower their eyes in response. Once more, the doctor questions them, "How could you have waited so long to come when you live so close?"

Without waiting for their response, he clicks his tongue in disgust. He gives instruction to his assistant, who he hastily dismisses with a sweep of his hands.

The aide gently motions for them to come with her. Without outward emotion, Laraba and Victoria follow her to the ward for children. The infants are placed in a bed together. Laraba sinks down to the floor. She closes her eyes and covers her face with her hands. She leans her back against the wall. From time to time, she opens one eye and looks between her fingers to watch what is to being done.

CHAPTER TWENTY

Two Coffins and a Letter

Audu begins another day in the city far from home. Each day he reflects on what has happened. How long has it been since that night? He has become less sure Laraba is in this town. But he must arise and seek more diligently.

As he walks in the market, it occurs to him that perhaps it's time to explore other areas of town. Though he doesn't know where he is going, he begins a journey down one of the main streets. In the distance, he sees some tall buildings. He questions what they hold and quickens his pace. Approaching one of the buildings, he sees a smaller structure to one side, as though set off to itself. Yet it is within the fence of the same compound.

Nearby, he also sees some carpenters busy with their tasks. They are working under a shed that protects them from the sun and rain. The ground inside is littered with wood shavings. There is only a path around the table where they walk or stand working. A stack of wood is nearby. It serves as a shelf for bags of nails and clamps, a tin of oil used to speed the saw on its way, and several different kinds of wood planes.

Two small boxes are on the table. They are only two and a half or three feet in length. They are soundly, though simply, constructed. Audu can't take his eyes off of them. As he nears the table, the carpenters warmly greet him. They think he might want them to do some work for him. "Good morning. How are you? May we help you?"

Audu asks, "What is the work that you are doing?"

"Is it not clear?"

"Yes, I can see."

"The wood is good. It is smooth and nailed tightly together," one of them says. "This is our work. We make tables, chairs, cabinets, and other things. We also make repairs on buildings. But we make these as well," he states, as he points to the two small coffins.

"Who are they for?" Audu is almost afraid to ask. He's not sure he can control his voice.

Audu remembers the twins on the ground under the tree. Often during the past weeks, he had tried to see them again in his mind. Whenever he began to bring them into focus, the blur was always there. Now, for the first time he sees them clearly. The coffins bring them into sharp focus.

"They lie there in the morgue beside the hospital," answers one of the skilled ones. He points toward the small cement block building to the back and left of the main hospital buildings. "For three pence the guard will let you look."

"Why would I want to look?" Audu asks defensively.

"Why did you ask who they are for if you are not interested?"

Audu doesn't answer quickly. When he speaks again, it is with a noticeable quiver in his voice. "It is not often that you see two small boxes being made. Is that not true?"

"It is true," the spokesman for the workers answers.

The silent carpenter takes a white cloth a little longer and wider than one of the coffins, and two inches or so from the top on one side of the box, he begins to tack it in place. He goes down the length of the coffin, nailing the material. Then he does the same thing on the other side of the box, being careful not to allow it to touch the bottom. He has prepared a hammock inside the box.

"What is that for?

"You do not know?"

"No."

"That will keep the body from touching the box. Is it not wise?"

Audu doesn't answer, but walks toward the morgue. The guard sits on a bench that leans against the wall of the building. He watches as Audu approaches.

"May I see the two? The small ones?" Audu requests in a low, almost inaudible voice.

"Are you to take them?" The keeper asks, as he stands up holding out his hands with palms turned upward. He had been told that the family of the twins had much money.

"No, I am not, but I must see them."

"You cannot see them."

Audu holds out his right hand. "This is for you. I must see them."

The watchman opens the door, as he pockets the coins. A cloth covers the bodies on a cement table near the center of the room. Audu blinks his eyes as the man turns on a light, which hangs over the table. Then he removes the cloth.

"Do you know them?"

Audu shakes his head and quickly leaves the room. He runs from the compound, deliberately avoiding the carpenters' shed. He realizes that those babies are newborns. His twins should be bigger and older. Tears slide down his face before he reaches the street. As he hurries away, the muscles tighten in his neck and shoulders. His whole body feels bound in some way. To whom had the two in the morgue belonged? Had they been killed, but are now to be buried? Again, he sees them on the cold, hard table.

Suddenly, his heart rejoices that he didn't take the lives of the two—his two babies. Had he not placed them under a large tree so that they would be protected from the sun and unseen spirits? Now he realizes that he had secretly wanted someone to find them and care for them. Hot tears stream down his face. Wiping them away with the hem of his garment, he discovers he is in a section of the city that is deserted at this hour.

Instead of going on toward the buildings of the city, Audu walks in the other direction. He comes to an area like the one where he had seen the men praying. There is an earthen pot. Removing the cover, he sees clean water. Beside the pot is an empty can. It appears to be clean also. He dips out some water and pours a little on the ground so the ancestors can drink first. It has been a long time since he's done this. After he quenches his thirst, he pours some water in his hands and washes his face. Covering the water pot, he places the can upside down so nothing can enter it. He sits on a large rock, deciding it is good to be alone. He needs to be quiet and still. He must consider what to do now.

Talking to himself, he whispers, "I have gone against the traditions of my family. But I do not regret that. Surely it is not wrong to keep the babies, even two of them."

He thinks about what he must do. So often he's discouraged and depressed. Still, he longs to find Laraba. He knows he needs to write

Uwa. Perhaps she'll have some news. Maybe he'll go to the cloth-seller's stall again. He hopes the man has returned and can help.

His thoughts return to the carpenters' shed and the morgue. Those babies must have been put into the river. Why were they rescued? What is the one doing now who had placed the two in the water?

Audu returns to his room with the conversation of the carpenters running through his mind. The horrible sight of the dead babies lying on the solid, cold cement causes chills to run up his spine. He thinks of his mother. She must be concerned and anxious to hear from him. He decides to write her right now. He takes his notebook and pencil to the table and begins this difficult task:

Dear Uwa and Roda:

Greetings from Danbar. The purpose of this letter is to tell you that I have not found Laraba. Have you had any word from her? As you so wisely said, 'all are strangers here.' Some of the people are friendly and kind. But all are strangers.

Audu's right hand is wet and cramped. It fails to move, as he seeks to place words on the paper. The decision to write had not been an easy one. Now, the laborious task is far more difficult than he had imagined.

Every night, I take heart and say to myself over and over, tomorrow things will be different. But it has not been so. My room is costing me one pound per month. It is a small room, but adequate. I have an electric light. The only thing that all have in common here is the desire for money. The city is a strange place. I will tell you about it when I return. I must keep looking. I know that I will find them. I trust you are both swimming in the ocean of good health. I will write again if I do not come soon.

Yours in desperation, Audu

P.S. Please get someone to write a letter for you. Send it to me at Box 246. This is the box of the man from whom I rent. Let me hear from you soon.

Audu walks wearily to the post office in the center of the town. He feels like an old man. He is tired. It's like he has spent years of toil and heartache. His pace is slow. His back aches. He can't imagine that this letter will bring good news back to him. Nevertheless, he should let his family know where he is. They need to know what he is doing. Uwa will have to get someone to read the letter to her, as she can't read. Some of the young men of the village will help her.

The post office is a large, concrete block building with many doors and windows. On the veranda sit a variety of people. One man has his goods strewn out for several feet in front of him. He sells oranges, onions, lemons, and carrots. Whenever a motor stops, he takes some choice merchandise to the person in the car. He tries to sell it. Before one has time to refuse to purchase with much vigor, he'll lower the cost a few pennies. Before long, he makes the prospective customer feel that a definite bargain is in store.

Almost blocking the main door, two traders sit with their imported wares of ballpoint pens, wristwatch bands made of synthetic leather and metal, sunglasses, stationery, and African-made wallets and small pocketbooks. As Audu approaches, one of the men stands up and goes to the steps. He holds out a shiny pen and some sheets of paper. "You will need these to write your next letter. I can give them to you for a good price."

Audu shakes his head. He continues up the stairs, almost stumbling into another man sitting on the top step. Beside him is his large basket of locally-made sandal thongs. This man also has some needle-point slippers to sell. Near the basket, there are a few handmade purses. He is ready to tell you of the fine leather and strong thread found in these items, as well as the good workmanship.

Several men and women beggars are sitting about, seeking assistance. Whenever anyone comes near, they reach out pleading for alms. One of the men seems to make this area his home. It doesn't matter when one goes to the post office; he is there.

Further away on the veranda of another building, but still a part of the complex, there are three or four "banana" women. Each declares hers are superior.

Audu enters the building. He gets in line to purchase a stamp. Later, the row of people reaches outside. The waiting will be long.

After being there about thirty minutes, he is the next to be served. In walk four men. They push in front of him. Before these leave, another comes and gets his stamps. Then the clerk disappears for her afternoon break. The rest of the customers can either wait or return later.

"Is this the way people act in the city? All I want is a stamp!"

A man behind him holds out a stamp, "Here, I have an extra one you may have."

"Thank you, you are very kind," Audu says, as he gives the man the correct change.

"Every time I come to the post office, I lose my patience," the man remarks.

Thanking the man again, Audu walks to the opposite counter to mail his letter.

◆ ◆ ◆ ◆ ◆

Several days pass before Uwa receives Audu's letter. From the time the envelope is torn open, she's in a daze. Removing the page terrifies this mother. She sends Roda for a scholar to read it. The boy comes. He reads to them. Haltingly, he pronounces the words. After concluding the letter, the lad quickly hands the open page and envelope back to Uwa. She receives it with trembling hands. Her heart aches, as she holds the paper. Fearing the results of this tragedy, the boy doesn't linger when he finishes.

Now Uwa sits on her stool. But she's no longer anxious. She has the news. She wants to speak, but what can she say? She holds back the tears that fill her eyes. She pulls her arms around herself and withdraws from all that is about her. Almost without ceasing, Uwa has thought of Audu, Laraba, and the twins. The pain of that night hadn't waned; the results are ever present. She now gives full attention to wondering about her lost ones. There are so many questions, so much anxiety. With the news, her apprehension reaches its high point.

Uwa's needs in life are simple. She was satisfied with Bako, the other wives, her children, and theirs. There had been disappointments, yes—but her compound is a place where others could come for support. Seldom before that night (a night never far from her mind) had there been times of such frustration and anxiety. Now these two feelings hover ever near.

Some in the village had begun to hold her responsible for every disappointment, every difficulty. This or that would never have happened, they say, if the curse of that night had been destroyed. Only yesterday, while walking in the market, Uwa had overheard another disturbing conversation.

"The rains stopped too soon," declared a women sitting beside her crate, with piles containing five or six red hot peppers for sale.

"We can blame Audu, his mother and his family for that. And has your farm had more insects than usual?"

"Oh my, yes! Another reason the twins should have been destroyed."

"You remember that Audu's mother was always too lax in her control over her children. They followed their own desires rather than the proven way of our elders."

"True," joined in another trader a few feet away.

"She offers too few sacrifices."

"I wonder about the cause of the evil that visited Audu and Laraba. Certainly there must have been a great act of disobedience for such a thing to have occurred," chimed in another woman.

Many tried to remember acts of defiance that either or both had committed. A man passing by stopped to remind them. "You will remember that we warned Audu that if he did not exert more control over Laraba there would be disaster. Now it has happened."

"Yes, is this not what is to be expected from a woman when too much is done for her?"

"He even did some of the work belonging to a woman. Perhaps that contributed to the wicked event."

"Why did he buy so much cloth for the expected child?" questioned a young woman who had been listening. "That was not proper!"

"How had Audu allowed Laraba to leave? He should have sent her away."

"How did she ever consider leaving? What would lead a wife to act as Laraba has done?"

Uwa quickly and quietly slips out of sight. She's careful not to show her feelings whenever she hears such talk. For a long time, she has known that any response would only bring more unfavorable comments and abuse. She had sacrificed several carefully chosen cocks. The goat that she offered was without blemish. The juju priest examined the animal and declared it acceptable. Everyone knows she had done this.

Few visit her compound now. Those who would come fear the criticism of the village. Even those who visit her are open and quick in their condemnation.

Uwa is proud of Audu. He's a good man. She's satisfied with the way she has taught him. He's well-trained. He works hard. He learned to be a man. Yet, he doesn't let his individuality keep him from respecting the group and their welfare. He has only half-heartedly supported the customs as they related to the supernatural and the many sacrifices. But he hasn't been arrogant or boisterous in this dissent. He hasn't questioned the actions and attitudes of others. Has he not shown tolerance of them? The twins had been taken without hesitation. Who knows what he did with the babies? What right did the villagers have to blame them for the trouble they now experience? During her life, she hasn't questioned the traditional beliefs of the elders that the birth of twins would be a curse to the compound and village of their birth.

Whenever she meets other women in the village, she pleads with her eyes. She only wants sympathy and understanding. Has she not suffered more than any in the loss of a son, the expected grandchild, and a dutiful daughter-in-law? What more could one lose? Hardest of all to bear now is the rejection of her people. She has given support to them. Now, their failure to reciprocate tears at her heart. Why, oh, why had her difficulties not brought sympathy for her? If they have felt any empathy, why have they not shown it to her?

Despair or Peace

Laraba and Victoria stand beside the twins' hospital bed. They stare into the babies' withered faces. They don't know what to expect. In his blue and white-striped uniform, the hospital aide returns. He holds a vial with a dropper. Gently, he squeezes several squirts into each baby's mouth. Then he turns to the women.

"I am sorry about your babies. This may help them."

"Thank you, thank you."

"We will do all we can for them."

Only Victoria responds. Laraba doesn't seem to hear either of them. She drops back to the floor and scoots up to the wall. Leaning back, she looks off into space. Victoria sits on the floor beside Laraba.

"Perhaps the medicine will help," Victoria softly tells her.

Laraba doesn't answer or look toward Victoria.

Victoria continues, "Try not to worry. I have seen babies like yours who were very sick respond to the treatment."

Laraba still doesn't say anything. She seems to be in shock. Her mind is overwhelmed, as she thinks. *I fear for my babies' lives. Going against my people's beliefs makes every minute anxious. This foreign city fills me with deep concern. Being in a strange hospital makes me apprehensive. Receiving that severe scolding about caring for my babies has been like taking a beating. Staying with people I have not known for very long is difficult. And sometimes I am unsure about them because they do not have all of my traditions. Despair and loneliness fill my heart.*

Victoria continues to try to comfort and assure her. But Laraba doesn't seem to hear what she says.

Although Victoria is reluctant to leave Laraba, she finally says, "I must go home to make food for John. It's almost time for him to go to work. I need to tell him about the babies. And his brothers will be hungry. I will return with food for you. I will also bring two sleeping mats and covers. We will want to sleep on the floor, one on each side of the bed."

Still, Laraba says nothing. She expresses no emotion. She seems to be numb to all that is around her. Whether the babies live or die doesn't appear to matter to her. Victoria quietly assures her, "I will return soon."

As Victoria leaves the hospital, she wonders if the infants will be alive when she returns. She hurries along her way to prepare the evening meal as quickly as possible. She knows in her heart that Laraba isn't ready to face the possibility of their death. Her apparent indifference is her way of coping with her situation. Many babies are stillborn or die soon after birth. One can't express grief for every death and difficulty, or one won't be able to withstand the trials of life.

Laraba sits quietly on the floor near the twins. Her mind continues to seek answers, to sort out recent events and conversations. Her thoughts return to that evening soon after her arrival in Danbar. It was when she and John had talked together. John had been sitting at the table reading a book. Laraba had entered the room. He had put the book aside to talk with her. She remembers in detail their conversation.

"The babies are asleep," she had said, smiling at him.

"I have been wanting to talk with you. We are glad you have come to our home. For as long as you wish, this will be home for you and your children."

"You do not fear the two? You do not think them evil?" Laraba's voice was calm.

"No, we know they are not evil. They are good. We believe they are a gift from God," John spoke with confidence. Laraba felt a sense of relief and joy that she hadn't known before.

"Laraba, I want to talk with you about something very important."

"I will hear."

"Why did you go to the bush and get the babies?" questioned her friend.

"Was it not the thing to do?"

"Yes, it was the thing to do," he answered reassuringly, "but why did you do it?"

"I wanted them. After they were taken from me, I knew a hurt that was not from their birth. My arms ached to hold my babies. Long I had carried them, but I had not held even one infant. My need for them was great. I could not control my going. I did what I had to do. Would not another do the same thing?"

"No, many have not done as you did."

"I would do it again. They are mine," she said with determination and certainty.

"It is the thing Victoria and I would have wanted you to do. We do not believe, as some do, that the birth of two is evil. We know they are not to be destroyed." After a few moments, John added, "Let me read you a very old story."

He picked up the book he had been reading and thumbed to the Old Testament. His fingers found the verse, and he almost quoted the words:

'And Isaac was forty years old when he took Rebekah to wife. And Isaac entreated The Lord for his wife, for she was barren. And the Lord was entreated of him, and Rebekah his wife conceived. And when her days to be delivered were fulfilled, behold, there were twins in her womb.'

John paused in his reading as Laraba questioned, "God gave the woman twins? What kind of god is that? Why would one write such a story?"

"Laraba, the God of Isaac is my God. He is the true God," answered John.

"How do you know him?" asked Laraba. "The gods of our people are not known. They are there in the grove or in the sky, but we do not know them."

"The God of this book," John said, as he held the Bible before her, "is the Living God. I want to tell you about him."

Laraba listened with interest, as John continued to tell her about the God of the book.

"This is a God of love—love for you and me. He sent His Son to die for us. All men and women have disobeyed, so God's Son paid for our disobedience."

"It is too much. How can this be? Who told you this story?" she asked, as disbelief and wonder shone in her eyes.

"Victoria and I believe in God. There are many other true stories to tell. Over and over again we have found strength in Jesus Christ, God's Son. He can meet your needs, too. That is the reason I have told you so much—I must go to work now, but we will talk again. There is much more that is good to tell."

After pondering this conversation with John, Laraba's thoughts turn to Audu. She is interrupted by the soft crying of one of the babies. Rising, she lifts it from the bed, and cradles it in her arms, rocking back and forth. It soon is quiet, so she puts it back in its place.

Again, she sits on the hospital floor and continues to think about Audu. *Surely he looked for me. Where is he? What is he doing? What is he thinking? Should I try to contact him?*

Laraba feels sure he had made a hurried trip to share the news with her father and mother. She could almost see him riding his cycle over the rough path. Her father would have asked Audu to come into the hut and sit. He would have called out, "Azumi, bring food. Audu has come." Her mother would have brought the food, though Audu probably couldn't eat it.

Father would have watched the path long after Audu cycled away. What did Father and Mother think when Audu told about the twins? Do not want to cause my parents to suffer. Some way I must let them know I am well.

Next, her thoughts turn to Uwa as she had last seen her. Her eyes were dark, tired, and strained. Her face held a wounded expression. Her silence was so uncharacteristic.

Know them all so well. Yet am not sure what they would do if they could see me now. Would Audu agree to keep the babies? Is that simply a dream? How would I be able to explain my actions? Is it best to wait? Will time help them to see? Or will the babies die here?

She decides she should talk to Victoria and John to help her determine what to do. They will only help. Neither will make the decision for her. At times, doubt about them had entered her mind. During these days in their home, she discovered that, in many ways, they were different from her and her family. But she also found she had been right and wise to come to them. Her impression during her first visit was correct. Victoria and John are what she had believed them to be. They are kind, thoughtful, and honest.

Victoria returns with food. Laraba looks up and smiles. Her kindness helps take away the anxiety and fear. Laraba hasn't left the hospital compound since she and Victoria brought the babies here. She won't leave until the babies recover or die. Whatever happens, she must stay with them.

◆　◆　◆　◆　◆

Laraba looks at the bowl of food and turns her head away. She puts her hands out to push it from her.

But Victoria coaches, "You must eat something."

"How can I? I am not hungry."

"We must take food so we will have the strength we need to take care of the babies during the night."

"My stomach aches already."

"How can you take care of your babies if you do not eat?"

Finally, Laraba takes a few small bites.

"Thank you for bringing the food. I know I need to eat."

Shortly after Victoria returns to the hospital, a young doctor comes in to examine the babies. With a warm smile, he begins to explain to Laraba and Victoria about the babies, "As you know they are very sick. They are very, very weak."

"Yes, yes, we know," replies Victoria.

Pointing to Laraba, he asks, "Are you the mother?"

"Yes, I am," she answers without fear. She realizes that no one has ever asked her that question before.

"The main problem is the lack of protein in their diets."

Seeing the blank expression on Laraba's face, he quickly adds, "The problem is that you are unable to produce enough milk for both of them."

Still, Laraba doesn't understand. Her questions aren't resolved. So, he states simply, "The infants are not getting enough of the right kind of food."

"What can be done to help them?" Victoria questions.

"While they are in the hospital, we'll give them the vitamins, milk, and whatever they need. If we aren't too late, we should soon notice some improvements. Then I will prepare a list of foods needed to ensure their growth and health. You won't find them too expensive or difficult to get," the doctor advises. "Day by day, I hope you will see some good changes."

"Thank you. Oh, thank you. We are very grateful," Laraba repeats several times, as she clasps her hands beneath her chin while tears of joy fill her eyes.

"I am a Christian and will be praying for their swift and complete recovery," replies the doctor.

Laraba and Victoria begin to smile.

"I know that you will care for them, though, as you well know, there are many who believe they are evil," said Victoria.

Laraba quickly glances at Victoria. By her expression Victoria sees she doesn't want the doctor to know her story.

"I must go now, but I will closely watch your babies," the physician encourages them as he leaves the room.

"Let us put down our mats and try to rest some. I know you are very tired. You did not sleep last night, and who knows what this night will bring,"

They lie down on either side of the babies' bed. Exhaustion allows Laraba to doze off.

CHAPTER TWENTY-TWO

Venturing Further

After another early morning roaming the open market looking for a brother, Audu decides to return to the center of the town where he had seen many big buildings. He comes to the largest one he has ever seen. It is five stories high. There are four double doors on three different streets. On every side there are tall windows. Though they are large and glass, you can't see inside the store. All that is visible are the things up close. There are different goods in each one—more things in each than are in most of the shops in the market at home. He stands watching the people entering and leaving the store. Those entering carry little. Those leaving carry bundles of goods. Most can't be identified because they are in cardboard boxes, paper bags or wrapped in paper. This isn't at all like purchases carried by those leaving the market in his village. There, everyone can see and know what a person buys even if it's wrapped loosely in leaves or sometimes in paper.

No longer can Audu control his curiosity. As nonchalantly as he can, he joins those entering the store. The first thing he sees is a set of stairs. Many of them are joined together. They move up towards an opening in the ceiling. People are standing on them and riding up. His eyes are as wide open as his mouth. He watches the people taking hold of the banisters and lugging their goods behind them as they get on the stairs. He has never seen nor imagined such a thing. He moves over to see them better. Someone bumps into him. He realizes he has stopped in the way and is staring at the moving stairs.

"Give me a chance to ride the escalator," an impatient woman demands, pushing past him.

People are everywhere. There are clear cases filled with goods and racks of clothing. Going on, he sees more bicycles than he has ever seen at one time. There are even several different sizes and colors. The only color he had ever seen before was black. Here there are also blue, red, and green ones.

Audu walks over into an empty spot next to a wall to be out of the way of the crowd. He stands there, baffled. He shakes his head to clear his mind. In a few moments he slips toward an area where food is being sold. He sees a door which opens into a very small room. Four or five people are standing in front of the door. As it opens, the ones waiting quickly enter, and the door closes. Over the door is a lighted area where he sees a two, then a three, a four, and a five. Even now, others are gathering before the door. Mesmerized, he watches the lighted area again, as he sees the five, four, three, two, and one. When the one appears, the door moves into the wall where it cannot be seen. The people in the room come out. Those waiting enter. The door closes.

Audu scratches his head. "What is this?" he whispers.

He has never seen so many people in one building. Yet not one is a friend he can greet. After walking slowly through the store again, he examines the goods. He looks at the people. Audu is bewildered and mystified. He passes through the double doors to the outside.

◆ ◆ ◆ ◆ ◆

Leaving the huge building, Audu goes back to the market area. After more fruitless meandering, he makes his way down one of the side streets. The dirty, rough road leading from the large busy market narrows between mud houses. Most of the dwellings have small windows made from tin. Old buckets had been flattened and cut to serve a new purpose. One of the houses is different. It is constructed of mud, but has been neatly painted. It has windows built of wood which are larger than those in the other houses. In front of this home is a eucalyptus tree. It is protected from the sheep and goats and the wood gatherers by some old, rusty barbed wire that had been wrapped around it several times when it first started growing. The tree has survived several dry seasons; now it seems sure to endure. It's easy to see this is a comfortable residence, unlike others on this street.

Next door is a building that once had been painted green. Now it's faded by the washes of many rains. Small glass panes outline the open double doors. One at the bottom had been broken but neatly replaced by thin plywood. A sign, "All Who Enter Are Welcome," catches Audu's attention. He reads the bottom line, which states that they meet every Sunday. After a moment's delay, he goes in. Exhausted, he takes a seat on one of the benches near the rear. It's on the right side, where the men are sitting. The women, in the majority, are on the left, with their babies tied on their backs. Small children are sitting or lying close together on grass mats near the front. An elderly man sits nearby, holding a long stick which he uses to tap any child who misbehaves.

"I'm pressing on to higher ground," is being sung with gusto.

Audu had never heard those words before. So he listens to them. He watches the people. What is the meaning of this, he wonders. These people seem happy, assured, and eager to declare their ideas to all who will listen. After the song, he sits down only to realize that everyone else is still standing. Quickly, he rises. He notices that all of the people have their heads dropped as if looking at the floor, but their eyes are closed. The one in charge speaks with his eyes closed. After he finishes talking, he says, "Amen." All of them sit down.

Audu turns to the man next to him and asks, "What did that man do? To whom was he speaking?"

With a surprised expression on his face, the man kindly replies, "He was talking to God. He asked God to help him as he talks to us." Audu finds all of this hard to understand.

The large, dark-skinned man in charge remains standing. Taking a big, black book in his hands, he says, "I am going to read you a story written by the doctor, Luke. This story tells us about an injured man. A doctor would know about such a man."

The speaker continues, "A lawyer asked Jesus, 'What must I do to have life without end?'"

Audu asks himself, "Life without end. What does this mean?"

"Jesus answered, 'You know the answer, you have the law.' The man replied, 'Love the Lord God with all of your heart, and with all your strength, and with all your mind, and your neighbor as yourself.'"

"Love the Lord God and your neighbor?" Audu wonders if that was really what he had heard. But he must keep up with what is being said.

"'You are right,' answered Jesus. 'Do this, and you will live.' But the lawyer was not satisfied. He asked, 'Who is my neighbor?'"

Audu wonders if the man will know the answer to this question also.

"You will remember that Jesus answered by telling this story. 'A man went from Jerusalem to Jericho. Thieves caught him and took all his goods and clothing. They beat him and left him half-dead. Three men then came along the road.' "

Now the speaker tells the rest of the story. "First, came a priest. When he neared the wounded man, he paused a safe distance away to look at him. Then he hurriedly passed on. We are surprised that he left without rendering assistance. You would expect him, being a man of the church, to help someone in need, wouldn't you?

"The second was a Levite, one who instructed people in the Biblical law. He had an important religious responsibility. As he came closer to the man, he stared with amazement at the crumpled, bleeding man. But, he too went by without helping him.

"The third person to approach the injured man was a Samaritan. He was from a different tribe than the wounded man. Their people despised each other. You would expect the Samaritan to leave his enemy unaided, but he went to the man. He poured oil into his wounds and covered them with cloths. He placed the man on his own donkey and walked along beside him to see that he did not fall off the animal. Soon, they came to an inn where the Samaritan left the man to recover. He also gave the caregiver money to take care of any other expenses.

"These three came to the same place on the road and saw an injured man. But they did not see the same thing. Only the Samaritan saw clearly a man in need and helped him. He saw a stranger, but also one desperate for compassion and care. He acted in love.

"There was another pair of eyes on the road, those of the beaten, robbed one. What did those tired, suffering, bewildered eyes see when they looked at the Priest and Levite? They saw unconcern, indifference, and fear in men who refused to come near, to touch or to treat. If they had any inward desire to help, it was resisted. Heads shaking, eyes downcast, those two walked away. First one and then the other. Rejection is the most difficult thing in all the world to accept from another human being. That's what filled the eyes seen by the hurt man.

"Then another set of eyes appeared. The injured man saw love and concern when the Samaritan helped him."

"Jesus asked the question, 'Who was the neighbor?'"

"It wasn't difficult to answer. 'The man who had compassion, the one who showed mercy.' "

"Then Jesus said to the lawyer, 'Go and you do the same thing,' "

"What meaning does this have for us?" asks the leader, looking around at the people gathered in the room.

"What do we see when we look at people? More importantly, what do they see when they look at us? It is not just what they see, but what we do.

"Many times each day, on the streets, in the market, we see those who need acceptance and help. We must act now. Opportunities are here for only a little while."

Audu had never heard such ideas. Too much had been asked. But he knows, having heard the questions, that he must find some answers. His mind won't stand still. He can't hold one thought because another races in to take its place. He is eager to know who Jesus is. He wants to know more about that man. He also wants to hear more stories about him. He wonders if Jesus will be able to help him. Many thoughts crowd into Audu's mind as he leaves. He walks like a sleep-walker in a stupor toward his room.

As he enters the house that now is his temporary home, he sees the old woman. She is sitting on a small, hand-carved stool. It had been intricately designed by burning the pattern into the wood. In her hand, she holds the beginning of a round grass mat. On the floor beside her, separated into piles, are long grass straws of different colors. With deft fingers, she selects a straw and skillfully enlarges the mat. She enjoys doing this task. The whole room is filled with her pleasure. She pauses in her quick movement, as she hears Audu approaching the entrance hall.

After placing the straws in the right order so she can find them according to their color, Taiwo, her devoted son, has gone to the market. Today, her pierced ears are adorned with earrings of twisted copper. Her head is covered with a bright red and green scarf. She calls out even before Audu enters the door.

"Welcome, Audu."

"How do you know who is here?" Audu asks, as he enters.

"I know. Every person has a different step. Your walk is different today. What happened?"

Audu is amazed at her perception. How could she possibly know what he had just experienced? It puzzles him. A goat skin is leaning in the corner. He unrolls it and sits down. He smiles as he watches the quick fingers. He is fascinated at her skill as she weaves the long straws into the mat. With every turn of the mat, he can easily follow the pattern in the design. Now, solemn in thought, he doesn't speak. Moments pass. Neither of them breaks the silence.

The old woman, busy with her work, gives even more attention to it. She respects Audu's silence. So she doesn't interrupt it. She reaches out, takes a long, red straw, and begins to weave it into the pattern of the mat. That one finished, she lifts a green one. She measures it by running her left hand down its length. Since only half of it is needed, it is broken.

Audu takes a kola nut from his pocket. He divides it into six pieces. "Here is kola," he says, reaching his hand out to the old woman. He carefully watches so he can put it in the palm of her hand.

"No, thank you," she speaks pleasantly, as she painstakingly chooses another straw.

Audu selects a piece of the broken nut. He begins to chew and doesn't speak until it is finished. Then words tumble out like a rushing river.

"Today, when I was leaving the market, I entered a large room. I do not know what drew me in. Singing filled the room. Others were coming in, too. On the wall was a sign, 'Welcome. You Are Invited To Join Us.' In front, two men sat on a platform. One of the men read words which the group then sang. The other man read from a large book. Then he talked about a story in that book. I have never heard such a story. It was interesting, but that was not the thing that drew and held my attention. The important thing was its teaching. Things I had never heard. But things I know. Every person knows them. There was nothing new. It was about the nature of people."

As best he can, he retells the story. He is no longer aware of the old woman busy with her weaving. Soon, he is lost in deep thought.

She listens to his words, but feels even more keenly his attitude. There is a fuller, more meaningful experience behind what he is saying.

"We do not all have the same nature, but we are all alike. Does it make sense? In the story, men responded like men, but the actions of men are unpredictable. Should it be so? Should people not act wisely and therefore properly? But who is to know what is wise?" Audu hesitates. Then he proceeds.

"Now I ask you, were the priest and Levite not wise to pass the man by? They did not know the cause of his difficulty. Did they rightly fear for themselves? Was it not possible that the ones who had attacked the man were hiding, waiting to rob and injure them? Did they not do right to move on quickly? There is much in this story. We cannot know it all. I think the man who told the story is trying to help those who hear him see in a deeper way than they have seen before." After a pause, Audu continues, "Until today, I have never thought about seeing."

"What do you mean?" asks the old one.

"I look with my eyes but only see a part of what I should see. For the first time, I am aware that I need to look more clearly."

"You see, but you do not see?" she asks.

"Yes. Today, the man kept asking the same question: 'What did he see?' I tried to imagine what each of them saw. Of course they saw a wounded man, but was there more to see? Now I realize that usually I do not look very deeply into things."

"I have been blind for a long, long time and I think I understand what you mean. I do not see with my eyes. But for one to say that I cannot see is wrong. I can see things that others do not see."

"Yes," replies Audu, "I understand what you are saying. I think Laraba saw things we did not understand, but we never talked about it. Why did we not talk?"

"Most of us wait too late to see and talk," the old woman answers.

Rolling up the goatskin, Audu places it back in the corner. Wishing the old woman a good night, he goes to his room. The dry hinges creak as he opens the door. He listens for the greeting. But what?

No sound from the bird? Apprehension overwhelms him. Rushing to the cage, he sees the golden tail feathers sticking out of the drinking bottle. The bird is dead. No water. No food. With disgust and anger, he throws the death house against the wall. When it doesn't completely break, he rushes over and stomps it. He can feel the wire and sticks give way beneath his weight. Seeds are scattered over the floor. He calls out, "No, no!" and drops to the floor, engulfed by fatigue.

The old woman hears the cry. Her first thought is to respond by going to Audu, but she thinks better of it and stays on her stool. There will be time to help him before he finds Laraba.

◆ ◆ ◆ ◆ ◆

Another unsuccessful week of wandering the market passages. Audu visits the letter-writers again, but they are unable to give any additional help. He goes to the cloth-seller, hoping to find he has returned.

"I have been here several times, but he is never there," Audu says to the trader in the adjoining booth. "Have you heard anything from him?"

"No, perhaps he is traveling."

Turning away, Audu scratches his head. He wonders where to go next. What to do? He doesn't think he will ever find Laraba without help from someone from home. He returns to his dull room, expecting another restless night.

The next morning, Audu remembers it is Sunday and goes back to the little church, eager to hear another story. This one is as interesting as the last ones had been. Audu is amazed that there are so many different tales that he had never heard. At home, the old men tell stories. They recall events of the olden days, of hunting, war, famine, marriage and death. They are interesting, but none of them had ever held his attention like these do. Although these are about other people, each is as personal as could be. Often Audu thinks this man, who does not know him, is talking directly to him. It's strange that this speaker knows about so many people and happenings. He's a good storyteller. But with such interesting stories, you don't have to be a teller of tales to capture and hold the attention of the listeners. Audu notices the other listeners are as fascinated as he is. It seems unusual that the stories come from a book. Even so, that doesn't make them any less intriguing.

"Where does the speaker find so many stories?" Audu asks a man, as they leave the meeting.

"They are from the Bible."

"What is the Bible?"

"It is a book telling the words of God."

"They are good stories. Everyone should hear them,"

"It is so."

"I want to get a Bible."

"You can get one from a bookseller in the market. Many sell them," shares the man. "We would like for you to join us in bible study at six o'clock in the morning. We meet here."

The next day, he arrives early. As they talk, Audu shares his frustration about not finding his wife and babies. One of the men takes him home with him for a meal, conversation, and prayer. Several offer to help him in his search. But no one knows anyone from his village.

"How can I help you?" asks this new friend, as they sit together to eat. "I am a tailor. Many people come to me in the market to make gowns or patch old clothes. Perhaps I can find someone from your village to help you."

"Would you do that for me?"

"Of course."

CHAPTER TWENTY-THREE

An Important Purchase

The thought of having a book with all those interesting stories intrigues Audu. He plans to read it until he knows the tales so he can tell them to those in his village. This is the only thing he has found with meaning in the city. This discovery makes him happy, but this isn't his purpose for being in Danbar. How can he find Laraba? She must be here somewhere. Where else could she have gone?

Returning to the place where he is staying, Audu is sad that the old woman isn't in the entrance hall. He wants to share with her what he had heard today. She seemed to enjoy the other things he had told her. But he doesn't want to disturb her by calling out. There's nothing else for him to do but go to his room. He shakes his head once more as he thinks about the latest tale. No matter what he's doing, these new stories he has heard during the past few weeks come to mind. He's glad he had entered the room that first day.

After resting for a while, Audu arises and goes outside. He decides to take a walk out of town down a road he'd heard about. He walks several miles until he comes to a small village. Seeing a woman grinding some dried field peas, he stops to watch her. Many times he has observed his mother and Laraba preparing the bread for their meals. He knows the peas must have been soaked in water long enough to be soft. The skin and black eyes are peeled off of them. The woman puts another handful of the peas on a large flat stone. She begins grinding them by pushing a smaller stone against the large one. The results are put in a wooden bowl. Salt, ground pepper, and finely-chopped onions are added. Gradually, a bit of water is mixed in. She beats it until it is light.

In a short time, the woman uses three fingers full of the mix to make small balls. She drops each in the hot palm oil. As Audu watches, he decides to purchase some to eat while it's hot. He licks his lips in anticipation of the delicious chin-chin. After bartering with the woman, he buys three balls of bread and walks away. As he eats, he longs to return to his village. He begins recalling many pleasant times there.

Soon, Audu doesn't see many other people on the road. To one side, he discovers some large rocks. He goes over to sit on one of them. It's quiet and peaceful. His mind returns to the sight of the two babies he had seen in the morgue. He wonders what he'd be doing now if Laraba had had only one baby. By now, they would have had the naming ceremony. But he is unclear what the name would have been, because he couldn't determine what circumstances would have been connected with its birth.

It would soon have been time to etch his tribal marks on the baby's face. Someone would have had to hold the baby's face taut. He must not move. Then the authorized man cuts the cheeks with a specially shaped and sharp knife. The skin would be pulled from the face. The marks need to be accurate. A certain kind of oil would be applied to keep the raw gashes open. This would make the scars permanent. As in the years gone by during the time of tribal wars, his baby would be identified as a member of his tribe. Audu's tender heart feels the pain a child experiences when the scars are put on its face. His hands go to his own face to feel his marks, and tears come to his eyes. Then he thinks he won't have a son as his heir at this time.

A renewed sense of grief at the disappearance of Laraba and the babies overwhelms him. Here, alone, he's free to let his hot tears pour down his face until his eyes are red. His body shakes, as he heaves for breath. He lifts the bottom of his long white garment to wipe his face and eyes. Many questions enter his mind.

He is bone weary. *What more can I do? Where can I go? Is there no help for me? Should I return home? What's happening there? What about Yahaya? Where is he? Is he still in jail or has he gotten out and is now looking for Laraba and the babies? What am I to do with the new beliefs I am forming?*

Audu crosses his arms on his knees and places his head on them. He can feel his knees trembling and wonders if he will be able to stand and walk back to his room. It's growing dark, so he needs to return to the town soon. He doesn't want to be caught out in the jungle where wild animals might be roaming around, or where some evil spirit can find him. He pushes himself up by using a smaller rock to his right side. Steadying himself, he starts down the road. Gradually, he picks up speed and reaches his empty room as dusk is ending.

◆　◆　◆　◆　◆

The next morning, Audu awakens early. His first thoughts are about the teaching of Jesus that he has learned. Lying on his bed, he talks to God as he had heard them do in the church. "God help me today in my search for Laraba and in my search to know more about you."

As soon as he can see light outside, he goes to a small building in the back of the compound to take a shower. Then he hurriedly leaves his room and quietly moves through the yard and entrance hall. No one in the compound is stirring. Only a few are on the street going to their work. He wonders if the food seller will be ready yet. So he walks leisurely down the narrow path to her stall.

"I will take food," Audu tells the girl from whom he often buys. The place is clean and close to where he is living, so it is convenient.

"The garri and okra soup are good. Do you want anything with it?"

"No, that will be all."

The girl serves Audu his food and hesitatingly begins to talk to him. "You are early this morning. There must be something important for you today?"

"Yes." He smiles. "I am going to buy a book."

"Buy a book?" she asks with interest. "I have never known anyone who was going to buy a book. What is it for?"

Audu laughs, "To read."

"Are you making fun of me?" The girl quickly turns and walks away. Audu begins to eat his food. He looks up and sees her watching him. He smiles as she walks back toward him.

"Are you serious? Is buying a book the important thing you have to do today?" she asks.

His excitement is expressed in explosive laughter. He realizes that it has been a long time since he had laughed at anything. It feels good. This moment of joy increases his eagerness to buy the book.

"Yes," he answers, "It is a book of many wonderful stories. Perhaps you know it. It is called the Bible."

"Yes, I have heard of it, but I cannot read, so I have no need of books."

"I have only learned about this book recently. I have not been interested in it until now. I have heard some of its stories. I want to read them for myself. Yes, I am going to buy a Bible."

He finishes eating and bids the girl good-bye. Then he walks quickly to the market. Often, he has passed the bookseller's stall on the way to look for Mai-zane, but this is the first time it has held any interest for him. Although he intends to make the purchase, he must be careful with the money he has left. Pausing before entering the stall, he examines several of the paperbacks on the table out front.

The salesman calls out, "That is an interesting one, but there are many more." He keeps on arranging his books, taking them from the boxes where he had stored them yesterday.

"I just want to see what you have," Audu declares, as he doesn't want to make his wishes known too soon, because he might have to pay more.

"I am sure you can find one which will interest you. Look well."

Audu doesn't see a Bible, but still isn't ready to ask for one. Examining several, he is amazed that books are so numerous.

After allowing Audu time to look carefully at some of his wares, the trader asks, "Are you looking for one book in particular?"

"Yes, but I do not see it."

"What is the name?"

"I am looking for a Bible."

"Please enter. I have several nice ones inside." The clerk leads the way. "They are here in this box." Picking up one, he says, "Here is a fine one. The cover is a certain kind of leather."

"It is nice, but I want a less expensive one."

"This is not expensive. I got it at a good price and I will sell it to you for a cheap price. You may have it for one pound."

"No, that is more than I can pay."

"Because this is your first visit to my shop, you may have it for eighteen shillings. Is it not good? Is it not a cheap, cheap price?"

"Yes, but show me another. One not so dear."

"I will show you another, but you will see that it cannot compare. This is the very best one," he says, holding the leather-bound one up.

Then he reaches into the box for a different one, a small paperback. He still has the first in his hand. Giving the new one to Audu, he states, "It is also a fine one, but not so fine as the first."

"What is your price?" Audu asks.

"You can see the paper is good and the printing is large and clear."

"Yes, but what is the price?"

"You are a new friend, so you can have this excellent one for only three shillings."

"Oh, that is still more than I can pay. I will give you one shilling."

"It is clear you do not understand the cost of books. One of this quality would never be so cheap. But you will be a good customer, so I will let you have it for two shillings."

"No, I must look elsewhere," Audu says, as he turns to leave, placing the book on the table.

"Do not go in haste. Look at it well," the shopkeeper begs, handing the Bible back to him.

"It is nice, but I cannot agree for such a price."

"What will you give for such a lovely Holy Book?" the trader asks in a very soft and reverent voice.

"I will give you one shilling, three pence."

"I can see you are going to be a good customer, so I will let you have it today for one shilling, six pence."

"You are very kind, but I can only pay one shilling, four pence. That is my last price."

"I will lose on that price, but since you are my first customer this morning, I will agree. I want you to buy all of your books from me."

Audu carefully counts out the money in his own hands, checking that it is correct, and then hands it to the bookseller with his right hand (to be sure not to offend).

Leaning slightly forward and reaching out for the money with both hands, the owner says, "Thank you, friend. You have kept me from making a profit, but you are my customer. I want to see you here often."

Audu hurries away, eager to begin his book. He looks for a place where he can sit without being disturbed. Not far from the market, he had seen a park with a few benches under a large, green, luxurious frangipani tree in full bloom with its red flowers. He goes there to begin reading the stories the preacher had told with elegance and emotion. He becomes so absorbed that he keeps reading all through the day. He reads slowly and often stops to think about what he has read. New ideas require consideration. From time to time, he looks up and rubs his eyes to relieve the tiredness. Normally he would have stopped for food, but not on this day.

At dusk, Audu returns to his room. Inside, he sits down in a chair beside the window. The remaining sunlight brightens the pages. He doesn't remember moving the chair near the table or turning on the electric light. Much later, he awakens. The book leaves are creased from the weight of his arms and head.

Quickly, he goes to the bucket outside and washes his face, running water over his eyes until they are clear. He closes and locks the window, noticing there's no moon. Taking a banana from a basket on the floor beside his bed, he returns to the table. Carefully, he smooths the pages and looks for his place. Marking the page with a stick, he peels the banana and returns to his reading as he eats. He is still hungry. One banana doesn't fill his empty stomach, so he gets another.

He reads and rereads until his eyes burn. Going again to the bucket, he washes them, letting the cool water bring refreshment. He dries his face and gets a drink of water, then makes his way to the latrine.

When he returns, he closes the Bible. Removing his pants and shirt, he takes his sleeping cloth from his box. After wrapping it about himself, he turns off the light and lies down. Sleep will not come. He thinks about Laraba and the two. Question after question troubles his mind, the most pressing being—*why can I not find them?*

Finally, slumber overcomes him, but he is awake before the first light. Arising, he goes to the latrine. It is chilly in the early morning. After drinking some water, he returns to his bed and draws his cloth close. As he lies down, he thinks about this new religion. Many thoughts fill his mind. He begins to pray. No longer does he repeat words he had heard at church. Now he speaks from his heart. Then he turns on the light and begins to read again. He doesn't understand some of it. Many of the names and words are strange to him. Soon, he dresses and leaves his room on his way to the market.

CHAPTER TWENTY-FOUR

A Fellow Villager Offers Help

Audu continues to worship and study with the congregation. Each time, he becomes better acquainted with them. Even though they are from several different people groups, he begins to feel more comfortable with them. He realizes that they possess something special. He decides he wants and needs that too. He believes what the pastor has said. More than that, he believes what he sees in the lives of the pastor and others who attend. They are different. They don't depend on the magic of the medicine man or woman. They don't offer sacrifices of goats and chickens, as his people do. A belief in a God of love who cares for them is a new and refreshing thought. They are kind, honest, friendly, loving, and helpful. He knows others who possess these attributes, but there's another quality these Christians have. They have problems, but they aren't defeated by them. Their faith in Christ is exemplified by love and assurance. That makes them different. He wants this difference in his life. But there are still questions he needs answered. He decides to speak to the preacher because he believes that man can help him.

◆ ◆ ◆ ◆ ◆

Several days have passed since Laraba and Victoria took the babies to the hospital. Now the little ones only lie there and seldom cry. When the doctor comes in to examine them, he simply shakes his head and says, "We will continue to treat them. I pray for them and for you."

Victoria places her arm about Laraba's trembling shoulders and says, "We will not give up yet."

"I know they are going to die. I should never have tried to save them."

"No, you did the right thing!"

Laraba turns from Victoria and stumbles over to the wall. Putting her hands out to catch herself, she leans her head against it, then she slides to the floor. Grabbing a corner of her wrap, she hides her eyes. With shaking hands, she covers her face, and wailing erupts from her lips.

Victoria doesn't know what to say. She has grown to love the babies as if they were her own. She sits down beside Laraba and places her hands over her own face as well.

◆ ◆ ◆ ◆ ◆

Audu trudges along staring at everyone he meets. *How many days have I walked these narrow paths in this market? Perhaps I need to go to another town to search. Perhaps tomorrow I will leave this place.* He considers returning home.

"Audu, Audu, is that you?"

He stops, transfixed by words spoken in his heart language. At first he doesn't recognize the voice. But the joy of hearing his name and his own language is as overwhelming as the harmattan dust that covers everything in its path before it is settled by the first rains. Entranced, he slowly turns, as Sidi runs up to him. His eyes are misty. His mouth is covered by a broad smile, as he takes Sidi's outstretched hand. Over and over again they swing their right arms out and quickly slap their hands together in the familiar hand claps of greeting.

"My brother, it is you?"

"Yes—and you! How good it is to see you."

In their village, the two men had not been close friends. But here in Danbar, each is what the other needs—someone from home. The two lonely men are in deep need of the support that only a fellow villager can give.

"How did you leave our people? It has been a long time since I have heard and many months since I left our village," remarks Sidi.

Audu realizes that Sidi doesn't know of his trouble. He wonders how he should answer him. But he replies, "All is well."

"When did you come? And what are you doing here?"

"I have been here only a short time," answers Audu, considering how much to tell his fellow tribesman.

"Come, let us go there and talk," Sidi says, pointing toward some benches under a large tree. A woman is selling food and drinks nearby.

"How good it is to hear my own language," states Audu, holding hands as they walk toward a shady place.

"A short time for you, but it has been a long time for me. I have seen few from home and none recently. We can talk freely here." Sidi points to a greasy, fly-spotted table.

"Bring us two sodas," requests Sidi, as he pays the woman behind the food stand.

After quenching his thirst, Audu speaks. "I do not know anyone from home who lives here. Do you?" He decides to take a slow approach in sharing about Laraba and the babies.

"Yes. I know many. But I have other good friends here too. Where are you living?" Sidi questions in his easy, pleasing voice.

"I have rented a small room on Block Street. The family has only one to let, so I am the only renter," answers Audu, as he watches a restless, black fly rub its feet together and then zoom from the speckled table.

"Three others share a room with me in a house where many strangers to Danbar live. Do you plan to remain here long?"

"I am here to find someone."

"It will be a job to find anyone in this city of many parts and many people. Whom do you seek?"

"This drink is refreshing," says Audu, avoiding the question.

"It is so," Sidi responds. Lifting his eyebrows, he turns to look at Audu with questioning eyes.

After a brief pause, Audu wearily begins, "My coming is a sad trip. The work I am here to do is unusual." He speaks so low that Sidi has to strain to hear him. Audu's nervousness disturbs Sidi. He regrets his persistence in seeking an answer as to why Audu is in Danbar.

Suddenly, Audu's words rush out, "My wife, Laraba, gave birth to twins. I took them to the forbidden bush. Then she disappeared. I think she must have recovered them. I have not been able to find her or the babies. That is why I am here." His voice breaks, as he cups his face in his hands.

As Audu speaks, Sidi shakes his head and clicks his tongue in utter disbelief. "The fear of twins no longer holds me in its grasp as it once did. In my travels, I have seen those with twins, who have accepted them as special." He comfortingly places his hands on Audu's arm as he suggests, "Let us go to my room. It is not far. I have a plan. We can talk there without being interrupted."

Rising, Audu glances about. No one is paying any attention to them. Sidi leads the way from the benches to the road. Neither of them speaks. Audu is oblivious to the bell-ringing cyclists. He doesn't even take note of the constant honking of an old taxi cab. Nor does he gaze at the faces of the crowd as they hurry along.

"We will soon be there."

Audu hears but doesn't answer. His thoughts are some other place. He doesn't know how far they have walked or how long it took them, when Sidi informs him, "This is where I live."

The house is big, well-built and has recently been painted white. There's a paved area in front of the building. A door to the entrance hall is open. No one is here. They move into the open courtyard. It's much larger than the front of the house indicates. Audu sees a small guava tree and a large mango tree. Two chairs sit in its shade. A small dog sleeps between the empty chairs. Many leaf stalks of the raffia palm are spread out on the ground to dry. Suddenly, three dragon-flies soar before them, up over the roof, causing Audu to smile. "That is a good sign," he chimes, pointing to the winged creatures.

"Yes, I am glad we are together," Sidi answers, as he takes keys from his pocket.

A stone fence about ten to twelve feet high encloses the yard. Like many city houses, when it was constructed, jagged edges of broken glass had been placed in the cement on the top of the wall to keep out thieves. A small concrete gutter goes under the wall, providing an easy path for the water, which pours off the roof during the heavy rains. The yard has been well-swept. Except for the drying palm, it's free of litter often found in such courtyards. A skinny yellow cat leisurely wanders into the courtyard from the entrance hall.

With one of the keys on his ring, Sidi unlocks the center door, which is painted dark green, blending well with the light green of the inside walls. The two windows in the room are closed. They too are painted dark-green. Sidi leads the way into the room, thus proving it was free of evil spirits.

"Come in," he speaks with a cheerful voice.

Audu enters, as Sidi goes over to open the windows on the opposite wall, the one that Audu had noticed from the outside. This huge room is neatly arranged and better furnished than any Audu has ever seen. It has a fluorescent light on the ceiling, and hanging from the light is a yellow strip of sticky paper about two and a half inches wide and eight inches long. He wonders if it is some kind of juju.

"What is that?" he asks, pointing toward the ceiling.

"It is a thing that kills mosquitoes and flies. They can worry a man here without protection."

There are four single beds, the metal, folding type, with a mosquito net for each of them. Audu had seen these nets in the market, but never hanging from the ceiling of a home.

He can't tell at first, but later he learns that the mattresses are foam rubber. A table with four chairs is near one wall. A lower table and four large chairs with cushions for the bottoms and backs are in the center of the room. By each bed is a locked box to hold clothing and personal items. The floor is covered with a bright-red, green, and black grass mat. An old calendar hangs on one wall.

"Have a seat," requests Sidi, as he leaves the room. "I will get us some refreshments and return shortly."

Audu sits in one of the comfortable chairs near the table. Sidi comes back with two bottles of warm soft drinks and a box of cookies. Taking a dish from the cupboard with a screen door, Sidi places the British biscuits on it and puts it on the table. He sits in one of the other chairs.

"If you feel like talking about Laraba and the babies, I would like to hear the story," pleads Sidi.

Audu takes his drink and holds it, looking at it intently as he turns it in his hands. Again, he feels the strain of that night. Sidi takes a swallow from his bottle and nibbles one of the sweets, as he waits for Audu to speak.

Without drinking, Audu begins, "I will tell you all that has happened. Then perhaps you can help me find Laraba, if she is in this city."

"I will listen and try to help," concludes Sidi, his eyes glued on Audu's face.

"We had looked with great anticipation to the coming of a child." Audu pauses. It's the first time he had spoken of the birth without thinking of a son. He relates the complete story, including his fruitless search. He also tells of meeting Yahaya, his loss of the money at the police station, and the experience with the money changer in the market.

"You have had much difficulty, but things will change now. I will help you. We will find Laraba and the babies. I do not want you to fear Yahaya. He talks a lot, but he will not do anything. It is late now, but we will plan. Tomorrow, we will begin looking for them early in the morning."

"Sidi, you are a good friend. But now, I have a question for you. I do not understand this room. It is different from any I have seen. How did you get it? What work do you do that would provide so much money? I know that this must cost plenty."

"Let's not talk about that now. There are more important things to do. We must find Laraba. There will be time for us to talk of other things later. Early in the morning, you return here, and we will begin our search. I have some friends who will help us. Here are two pounds. That will replace some of your lost money."

"Thank you. You are a true brother to help me in my time of great need," confirms Audu.

After receiving directions to his room and back, Audu carefully notices the location of Sidi's house. He doesn't want to have trouble finding it tomorrow. As he departs, he walks fast and smiles to himself. He is in high spirits. This is the first real encouragement he has received since coming to Danbar. Now there is hope of getting help to find Laraba and his babies.

◆ ◆ ◆ ◆ ◆

When Audu opens the window to his room the next day, he looks up toward the sky, which is especially bright and blue. "This will be a good day," he mutters aloud, as he hurriedly leaves.

He can hardly wait to reach Sidi's room. Arriving, he sees many people milling around in front of the compound where Sidi lives.

There are two police bicycles and a number of officers roaming around the compound.

Audu trembles, as he asks a man standing on the edge of the crowd, "What has happened?"

"I am not sure, but they say that four men who live in there," he points to Sidi's compound, "have been arrested."

"What did they do?" gasps Audu.

"They are saying that they are engaged in taking strong young men and selling them to work in the mines in Makaland. It seems that they would, under one pretense or another, lead them to the out-skirts of the city. There, in a remote place, some men from Makaland pay them and take the workers away. I do not know how the police found out about it."

Five officers come out of the door with Sidi and three other well-dressed young men. Audu watches with startled eyes. He's too terri-fied to speak. Fear causes his body to sag; his strength seems to leave him. He strains, putting forth his utmost effort to control his emo-tions. The hope, envisioned just a few minutes ago, is shattered.

As he shuffles through the streets back to his room, he shakes his head and mutters, "Why? Why?"

Gradually, his fear and distress over Sidi begin to subside. He gains a feeling of confidence. There's still time to find Laraba and the babies.

◆ ◆ ◆ ◆ ◆

Going into the house, he sees the old blind woman sitting in her usual place in the entrance hall. The pain etched on her scarred, tired face enters Audu's mind. It becomes a part of him. He's wounded by the desperation that crowds in the room.

For the first time in many weeks, he has concern for someone other than himself. Now he feels the suffering of another person. His hopelessness is gone for the time being, but the sadness of another more than fills its place. He isn't aware of the cause of her despondency, but feels the despair that is here. On a small stool, he sits down, not speaking, but sharing in her suffering.

The elderly woman begins to rock back and forth. It's so slow at first that the movement can only be felt, not seen. Her shaking grad-ually becomes intense. It only subsides as tears flow from the bizarre sockets. Audu doesn't speak, but he feels droplets run down his own face. Her tears have become his own.

"He is dead. My son is dead," she wails.

What can he say? How can one console?

"He was wounded by the soldiers. I did not know he was hurt." She can't stop weeping. "Now he is dead, far away—dead and buried."

Audu doesn't have any idea what she is talking about, yet he can join in her suffering. Taiwo is the only son he knows about. He is at work. In their talks, she had never mentioned another son. There's nothing he can say. She is silent. The tears cease. The slow movement begins again. Audu remains seated in front of her, feeling uneasy. What right does he have to be here in the midst of her suffering? Yet he doesn't have the strength to lift himself up and leave. He can't walk through the hall to his own room. He will just have to wait until she shares enough for him to say something.

It is several minutes before the grieving woman speaks again. "So long ago he went away. He was never satisfied here. The restlessness of youth consumed him. He could not be still. He paced the city as other men pace a room. He could not remain in one place for very long. He was not like his father or his twin brother, Taiwo, or anyone I have ever known. Now he is gone."

Audu is surprised to learn that this one he has become fond of is the mother of twins. Finally, he dares to speak, "May you know peace." After pausing a moment, he gently questions, "Where did this terrible thing happen?"

"Here," the old woman thrusts toward him a tear soaked letter she's been clutching.

He takes it. Carefully, he begins to smooth out the envelope. He removes the crumpled sheet and presses the wrinkles from the paper. Audu reads silently:

Komo Association
Box 432, Lakare
23 July

Dear Sister from Komo:

We, the people of Komo now living in Lakare, regret to have to share this sad news with you and your friends from Komo living in

Danbar. We all are grieving with you. On Saturday the 17th Kehinde was passing the Government House when a lorry loaded with soldiers arrived. It was by chance that he was passing that way. When the soldiers from the lorry and the guards in the Government House began to shoot their guns, Kehinde was hit. We do not know who shot the gun that wounded him, whether it was the soldiers outside the fence or the guards inside. It does not matter now. He was taken to the hospital when it was over. One from Komo working in the hospital informed the Komo Association that he was there. We went to offer help, but we were told he had died. It was so. We of your place buried him. Many from Komo were present. All are sad. We are sorry to have to write you such news. It makes our hearts hurt.

Your brothers and sisters from Komo
Chairman of the Komo Association in Lakare

Audu doesn't speak for a moment. After reading the letter, he looks curiously at the old woman. He thinks someone must have read the letter to her. Who would do that to a mother and leave her alone? Wouldn't that be cruel? On the other hand, perhaps that was the wise thing to do.

"Why was he buried away from our home? Away from our people?" she hesitatingly questions. She bows her head to catch her tears with unsteady hands.

Lines of anger form around Audu's eyes. His lips become rigid. His mouth is dry. During the past few moments, in this room filled with grief, he has learned more than he had previously known about the old woman. Why does he know so little about her? He sees his own selfishness. Often they have talked, but every time it was his interests, his life, and his problems that they discussed. He realizes now that he can't help her because he doesn't really know her. He quivers, as tears cloud his eyes. That helps ease his pain—the aching of awareness.

She hears his crying and seeks to comfort him. "I will know peace," she assures him. "The loss hurts, but time will help. You should not weep. Comfort will come to you."

Again, she helps me. Audu is amazed at the thought.

CHAPTER TWENTY-FIVE

Finally, Peace

The following morning, when Audu awakens he prays. This is becoming his custom. He seeks strength for the day and understanding about what happened with Sidi. Then he remembers the old woman and her grief. "Show me ways to comfort her," he whispers.

After dressing, Audu goes from his room through the entrance hall to the street. Light, quickly dancing clouds enhance the beauty of a blue sky brightened by the brilliant sun. Many birds of various colors and sizes flit about, searching for food in an empty lot across the street from his room. The grass and trees, in different shades of green, are caught by the light breeze and mark a path down the road. It's a pleasant, peaceful morning. Some people have moved from their cramped quarters to the open air, where they now lounge on multicolored mats on the ground.

Going down the street, he sees a young woman carrying a small box on her head. The lower calves of her legs are smeared with ochre giving them a glow. Audu notices her with pleasure. The red ochre is a common sight in his village. He wonders why it isn't used more often by the women of the city. Almost inaudibly, he speaks a morning greeting as they pass each other. Pleasantly, she answers without slowing her pace. Audu turns and watches her until she is out of sight.

The city offers many problems for one recently from the village. The only benefit he has found here is the church and its message. Today, he has a new purpose. He quickens his step. Gone is the restlessness of the previous days. He knows where he's going and why. Though he hasn't found Laraba in the city, he has found something he didn't know before. It's sad to him that he hadn't learned its teachings many years earlier. Few, if any, in his village know what he has discovered in the past few weeks. He wishes he could share this good news with them and especially with Laraba.

In the midst of all his excitement, his eagerness to find her has only increased. He feels more confidence about that now than previously. Audu wonders how he would introduce Laraba to his new faith. How would she respond to this message of love? It's so very different from what they'd always known. Instead of gods who must be appeased so they will not harm you, he now worships God, who cares about people. It's pleasant to ponder Laraba's response. He prays for strength and direction. This new experience of prayer is having a great effect upon his life. He's certain that it will bring a successful end to his search for precious Laraba.

With joy and anticipation about the story he'll hear this time, he walks to the place of worship near the market. He first found it by accident, but his visits now are deliberate. They are filled with expectation. What new ideas will be brought to his mind today?

Many are entering the church when Audu arrives. "Good morning. How are you?" he says to a man with whom he has discussed some of his problems and questions.

"Fine, and you?"

"All is well. How is your family? How is your work?" Audu questions another friend.

His greetings are returned heartily, as he speaks to those he has talked with before. He takes his place on the right, next to two young men. Placing his Bible by his side on the bench, he bows his head. As others enter the room, they too pray silently before the service begins. This comes as naturally to Audu, after only a few weeks, as if he'd been doing it most of his life. After a brief but deeply sincere prayer, Audu notices that the chair usually occupied by the preacher is taken by a stranger. He doesn't know this man, so he feels uneasy. He had hoped to speak with the other leader, who has been used by God to reach him. His anxiety soon passes, as the stranger stands to speak. His voice is strong and clear. His bearing is compassionate and sincere.

The preacher begins by asking, "Where are you?"

As he speaks, his deep voice rings through the room. The words bounce from wall to wall, running here and there finding the ears of the listeners. "The Lord God asked Adam this in the Garden of Eden. He asks you and me the same thing. Do you hear him?"

Though Audu doesn't audibly answer, a contented smile brightens his face. Then he whispers to himself, "Yes, I know where I am now. I want to be a follower of Jesus."

As the preacher continues, perspiration covers his face. Briefly he silently stares off into space. He seems to ponder his own relationships even as he requests the congregation to do so.

Suddenly, the baby on the back of a woman sitting on the bench across from Audu begins to squirm and cries out. The mother quickly stands up and adjusts her wrap around the small one. She slips outside. Audu wishes it were Laraba sitting in church with their twins. He wonders how she would manage two instead of one.

Audu's attention is brought back to the sermon, as he hears the people saying, "Amen." The speaker wipes his face with a clean, white cloth as the perspiration ceases flowing. The audience sits on the edges of the benches, their eyes fastened on the preacher's face. Intense interest causes some to lean forward, as if to hear more clearly.

"Let us look at the question with its many paths—turn it this way and that as a confused wind turns a leaf. Where are you in relation to your family?

"No one can answer for you. Husband, where are you in relation to your wife? Wife, where are you in relation to your husband? Is it fair to ask? You do not have to express your thoughts to others, but know your answer."

Audu wonders where the man will go now. What more can be added? He feels the fast pounding of his heart. He looks down at his shirt to see if the movement is noticeable. He begins to tremble.

"Where are you in relation to others?" The pastor continues.

Audu hears the question, but he isn't ready to leave the previous one. He wants to speak out, "Wait. I am not finished." Although the minister goes on, Audu continues to carefully explore the one about the relation to one's wife. This is what he wants to know!

His thoughts return to the message when he hears, "What is your relationship to God?"

This perplexes Audu. He shakes his head and wonders what other things have been asked that he failed to hear.

The speaker proceeds, "In the New Testament book of Matthew, we read the question, 'What think you of Christ?' The question,

'Where are you in relation to God?' cannot be answered until you answer this. 'What do you think of Jesus, who is called Christ?' We know that Jesus is God's Son, and we must look to Him for forgiveness and strength."

Audu's mind can't catch and hold all of these ideas. He pounces on one, but it slips from his grasp. There is much to think about.

He's learned that, to be a Christian, one must admit that he is a sinner and that God's Son is the one who forgives sin. He knows he needs to be forgiven for his mean thoughts. His hate of Yahaya has been gnawing at him and must be released. It's difficult to pardon the money changer and the police who have robbed him. Yet he knows his anger, resentment, and fear must be given up. He'll speak to the preacher after the sermon.

The message is short and plain. It is filled with thoughtful questions and clear ideas. As the hymn of invitation "Follow, Follow, I Will Follow Jesus" is sung, Audu moves toward the leader. He's amazed that he can stand and walk in front of so many people. He is confident he knows what he will do with Jesus. A joy that he hadn't thought possible brings a smile to his face. Peace floods his mind and heart.

As the pastor takes Audu's hand, he says, "We are glad you have come." In a soft voice filled with concern and encouragement, he asks, "Will you please share your decision?"

"Yes," Audu responds. "I want to declare my faith in Jesus. I believe. I have heard the message several times. I have a Bible. I have been studying the New Testament. Matthew, Mark, Luke, and John have taught me so much. There is much I do not know or understand, but I do know I believe in Jesus Christ as my Savior."

"Good. Let me tell the others what you have said. They will also be happy for you."

When he shares with the people what Audu has told him, many smile and clap their hands. Some murmur, "It is good."

Turning to Audu, he says warmly, "After we pray, we will talk. I am John. I want to get to know you."

After the prayer, many come by and speak to Audu. "I am happy you have become a Christian," says one man.

"What you have decided is good."

After the crowd leaves, John and Audu sit on one of the benches talking.

"Is Danbar your home?" asks the preacher.

"No. I am from Barikin Biyu."

"What brought you to the city?"

Words tumble out of Audu's mouth like a flood. He tells John the full story. John listens intently, as the words roll from Audu's lips. He keeps clicking his tongue, indicating his surprise at Audu's story. Several times he stands up, then sits down again. He can hardly believe the words he hears.

"And where did you say you are from?" John asks again.

"I am from Barikin Biyu and have lived there my entire life. This is my first trip so far away from my home."

"Tell me again the name of your wife."

"Laraba."

John bursts out laughing and claps his hands, "Audu, Laraba and the twins are with us. She found the babies and brought them to my house. They are now with my wife, Victoria."

Audu leaps to his feet. His whole body trembles. "What are you saying?" he asks eagerly. "Did you really say you know Laraba and the twins? You know them? They are with you?" His voice breaks, as he sobs, "It cannot be so! Can it be true that I have found them?" Perspiration forms on his brow. He looks at John with large, questioning eyes, astonished and confused.

"Yes," John comforts him, "They are with me. They were to be here. I do not know why they did not come. Let us go to my house, so you can see them with your own eyes."

"You mean Laraba planned to come here—to church?"

"Yes, Laraba has become a Christian."

"It is too wonderful to be true." Audu shakes his head and drops back down on his bench, wiping the tears from his eyes.

"Come. Let us go to them now," John's voice cracks, as he turns toward the door.

John starts out of the church. Audu quickly follows. Down the street they see a throng of people milling around. Three police officers, dressed in navy blue knickers and white shirts, are busy with a tape. Bending over, they are measuring the length of tire marks on the road. Several motors are parked nearby. Beyond the crowd is a lorry. It has crossed the ditch and crashed against a wall.

"What happened?" John asks.

"An accident. The lorry went out of control, ran over the ditch, and across the footpath. It hit several people. One woman and a baby were killed. Another woman with a baby was taken to the hospital. Others also have been taken there. The police are looking for the driver. He ran away after the accident."

Neither Audu nor John say anything for a moment. Then they look at each other as both of them ask at once, "Could it be Laraba and the twins?"

John turns to the man who told them what had happened. "Do you know who they were?"

"No. I have not heard anyone else say that they know them either."

"Excuse me, excuse me, I must pass!" Audu calls out as they push through the crowd to try to find out who had been in the accident.

Reaching the motor turned on its side, John asks the officer, "Who was hurt?"

"I do not know them."

Several people either sit leaning against a tree or lie on the ground. Some are moaning. One is bleeding from the leg. Audu stops near a man stretched out on the ground. He gurgles, as blood oozes from his mouth.

"I heard someone say he was looking for a woman with twins," a woman standing nearby interjects.

Audu gasps, as he looks closer. He sees the man's tribal marks and recognizes Yahaya.

"John, come—look! It is the juju priest's son from home."

As they stare at him, the policeman says, "He is dying. There was no reason to take him to the hospital. They will soon take him to the morgue."

John looks around and says, "Audu, I do not see anyone familiar here. Let us go to the house and see if they are there."

Audu clicks his tongue and shakes his head. There is nothing to say. For days he has been looking into the faces of people in the market and on the streets. He has seen all kinds of expressions. But none had a face as worried as John's, as they hurry from the scene of the accident. With deep furrows in his forehead and his lips pressed together in almost a straight line, John runs along the road.

Calling over his shoulder, he says, "We must not panic or jump to any conclusions. But we must hurry." His voice becomes so low Audu can hardly hear him.

They reach the house. The door is locked. John speaks to a neighbor, who is sitting in front of the next house. "Have you seen Victoria and our friends?"

"Yes, I saw them leave some time ago. I think they were going to the church."

"Quickly, let us go to the hospital," John says, as he turns and trots down the road. Their hearts are racing—dreading what they might learn there.

Almost out of breath, they reach the medical compound, which contains several faded white buildings. The main gate is open. John knows the guard, who is stationed at the entrance. He sits on a chair, leaning against the fence, and pays little attention to those coming and going.

John often visits patients and their families here. As he and Audu go through the opening, John calls to his friend, "Have you seen Victoria pass this way?"

"No. Is there trouble?"

"I do not know. We are trying to find her."

They almost bump into a food seller who is hawking her goods to those standing around. Many others have brought meals for patients, since it is the responsibility of family members to supply their food.

John leads the way. Audu follows closely behind. They quickly move to the emergency building. There are two parts in this section. The first room was too small, so additional space had been added. John knows that he and Audu will not be allowed to enter. He will ask if Victoria, Laraba, and the children are here. There are only a few people in the area, which is rare. He looks around but doesn't know any of them. He seeks a hospital attendant to ask who is inside. No one appears.

Each ER wing has a window. Few are bold enough to look in. John's anxiety doesn't hamper him. Without further hesitation, he slips up, stands on his tiptoes, and peers through the small glass in the door to one of the emergency rooms. There are three in white working over someone on the table. He cannot see clearly, but he can tell that it's a man. Audu watches John and sees no change in his expression, as he stares into the room. Without a word, John moves down the building toward the other window. Looking in, he discovers an empty room.

Turning to Audu, John says, "They are not here." Seeing Audu's wide eyes and raised eyebrows, he adds, "Come, we will look elsewhere."

Audu's throat is so constricted, he can't speak. He feels weakness in the pit of his stomach. He finds it difficult to keep up with John, who walks rapidly on. They go toward the center of the hospital compound. At the end of a long building, they turn a corner and see a woman with a baby on her back. Her left arm is bandaged with white cloth.

"Victoria! Victoria!" John calls anxiously, "You are here! Are you badly hurt?"

She shakes her head.

"Where is Laraba?"

"Come," she says without answering his questions. "Who do you have with you?"

"This is Audu."

"Where did you find him?"

"At church."

John and Audu hurry and soon are at her side. Together they have entered a large waiting room. Though there are many in the room, they immediately spot Laraba. Her back is turned toward them and on it is a baby. One of Laraba's legs is in a cast, but no other injury is apparent.

"Laraba! Laraba!" Victoria calls out to her, above the loud noises of the room.

Laraba turns and sees Audu and John. She trembles and gasps, as both of her hands fly to cover her face, trying to hide her fear. Will he still kill the twins? But she whispers, with a sigh of relief, "Thank you, God, we have been found."

Quickly, Audu goes and kneels beside her. "Oh, Laraba, are you all right? Let me see the baby." She turns so her back is toward him. He pulls away the cloth holding the brown-eyed infant and gently smooths its black, curly, hair as he peers into its soft, dark face.

"But what about the other one?" he asks, catching his breath.

"Look on Victoria's back."

Wheeling around, he smiles, as he stares at that baby. Victoria unwraps the little one and puts it into Audu's outstretched arms. Tears wet his eyes, as he draws his infant close to himself.

Victoria says to John, "Before you came, I was getting ready to find a taxi. Laraba cannot walk as far as our house."

"I will get one. We can all return home together. When you see the motor coming, you and Audu help Laraba out. With success I will return in a few minutes. We all have many questions. We want to hear every answer."

John runs toward the main gate. His friend, the guard, helps him secure a taxi. Audu returns to Laraba's side. He squats down and speaks quietly, "It has been so long. I have searched and searched for you. Many days and nights I have spent in agony. Now, my search is over! The grace of God has brought us back together. Are you sure you are all right?"

"Yes, do not worry. I have longed for you—but I feared for the babies."

"You need no longer fear for them because of me. I have become a Christian. I have learned many things, though there is still much I do not know. I no longer fear twins. Together, we, you and I, shall care for the babies. We will find a way. It will not be easy, but with God's help, we shall succeed. "The power of the two babies will not destroy us. Rather, it will strengthen us."

Suddenly, both of them are weeping and speaking at once. Laraba questions, "Audu, how did you learn about Jesus? How did you meet John?"

Audu didn't hear her questions, as he is asking, "When did you become a Christian? What made you go to find John and Victoria? How did you get to Danbar?"

With a release of pent-up fear, worry, and tension, they look at each other, dry their tears, and begin to laugh loudly. "Yes, I know," Audu said, "Our stories are long. There is so much I wish to know."

"I, also," Laraba agrees.

Holding one baby with one arm, Audu puts the other around Laraba's waist and helps her get up. She reaches back to steady the child on her back. He whispers to her, "I love you and thank God you saved our babies. They are priceless! We wondered if we would even have one baby. Now God has blessed us with two children. I am so happy."

udu and Laraba realize they can't return home with the twins. Their fellow tribesmen would either secretively or boldly kill the infants. But they can't continue to live with John and Victoria.

A few days after Audu finds Laraba and the twins, John's friend Ali, the night watchman returns to his home in the bush to care for his parents. He gives his employer the usual two weeks' notice. John recommends Audu for the job. The owner interviews and hires him.

As Audu, Laraba, John and Victoria discuss what to do, Audu determines that he must return home to share with Uwa that he and his family are safe. He will offer for her to come live with them in the city, but he's certain she won't agree. In that case, he'll promise his mother to return home when the babies are older. They pray that by then, it will be evident that the children are not evil.

Because their faith in Jesus Christ gives them an abiding peace and joy in their lives, Audu and Laraba discuss how to best tell Uwa about this. They are certain her life will be happier if she too believes. Both feel compelled to do this now, especially since she's an old woman.

After a short period of time at home, Audu plans to gather together their clothes, money, sleeping mats, stools, his bicycle, and as many of their other possessions as possible. He hopes to be able to harvest some of the last of Laraba's maize. It will be fully matured and hard, just as they like it. When he returns to Danbar, he'll find a small place for them to live.

Like Uwa, Laraba's parents believe twins are evil. Therefore, it's not safe for her to go home with the babies. Since she wants her parents to know about their welfare and their faith, Audu will stop in their village on his way to see his mother. He will attempt to determine if Laraba and the twins could visit them without apprehension. While there, he will share his faith with them.

One other person Audu remembers is his blind, elderly friend. He tells Laraba about her. He wants to take his wife and the children for her to get to know.

Audu and Laraba realize it may be a long time before they can return to their parents' homes with their babies. But they are satisfied with the prospects of a different life, home, job and new friends in this city. This is where they both have faced and overcome anxiety and frustration. Best of all, they have each other, their lively twins, and a growing faith in Jesus as their Savior and Lord.

Bob and Jo Ann Parham were educated at the University of Florida and Southern Baptist Theological Seminary. They served as missionaries in Nigeria from 1953-1974. After Bob developed MS, he was required to rest daily. It was at that time that he began writing the story of *The Power of Two*. Jo Ann completed the story years later.